Praise for

To the Children of Light

The title, *To The Children of Light* reveals not only the content of the book but Thomas's heart and style. He has a burdened to share his heart with his fellow believers. He does so in a conversational manner as if involved in a one-on-one, heart-to-heart chat. Simultaneously, he addresses the Church in general the church at large, the local church, leaders in the church, people of the pew, and even himself. It is clear that he loves the Lord with all his heart, cares deeply about the people, and is fully committed to the ministry as a service to Christ and people. In everything he shares, he invokes the Scriptures as the foundation and burden. Though not explicitly mentioned, his message is one of getting back to the basics of Christianity -- love of God, obeying His word, serving Him all out, loving the family of God, and reaching out to the lost. It is heartening to see one of this generation so committed to living true Christianity and to leading and inspiring others to do likewise.

—**Rev. Clifford Hurst**, M.A., *Ozark Bible Institute Instructor and Academic Dean*

***

To The Children of Light, a much-needed shaking of the shoulders to the modern church. It is a wakeup call to return to the authority of Scripture and the fullness of the Holy Ghost. Within these pages, you will find clear doctrinal and practical applications drawn straight from the Word of God and the life experience of a faithful pastor. This is not theoretical; it's a lived theology.

Pastor Hammond reminds us that the Church is still the Bride of Christ, called to shine bright in these dark days. If you are hungry for more than just "Americanized Christianity..." if you have a desire to see the Church return, not to the 1940s or 50s, but all the way back to the book of Acts of the Apostles, I believe To The Children of Light is required reading.
—**Rev. Jeremy Pinson**, Bible Holiness Youth Pastor, *Ozark Bible Institute Instructor*

***

Thank you, Pastor Hammond, for such a timely reminder of the absolute importance of and adherence to the Word of God! Never before has there been a need for the church to recognize that we live in an hour that "truth has fallen in the streets" than right now. We must rise up as Children of Light with knowledge and zeal for that truth, that this generation may experience the fact that the truth "shall make you free!"

—Rev. Andy Stringfellow

***

In, *To The Children of Light*, Pastor Hammond offers a rare blend of biblical clarity, pastoral warmth, and Pentecostal conviction. This book calls the church back to its first principles—sound doctrine, genuine conversion, Spirit-led holiness, courageous leadership, loving discipline, and Great Commission urgency—while offering practical pathways for believers and congregations to live them out. I commend this work to pastors, students, and lay leaders who long to see the Pentecostal church flourish—rooted in truth, alive in the Spirit, and shining as children of light.

—**Dr. Timothy Laurito**, D.Min. *Southwestern Assembly of God University*, Pastor of *Bible Holiness Assembly of God*, and President of *Ozark Bible Institute and College*

TO THE CHILDREN OF LIGHT

Exposing Shadows, Restoring Truth

THOMAS REED HAMMOND, JR

Published by KHARIS PUBLISHING, an imprint of KHARIS MEDIA LLC.

ISBN-13: 978-1-63746-672-8

ISBN-10: 1-63746-672-2

Library of Congress Control Number: 2026935287

Unless otherwise indicated, all Scripture provided in the Scripture quotations, unless otherwise noted, are from the King James Version.

All KHARIS PUBLISHING products are available at special quantity discounts for bulk purchases for sales promotions, premiums, fund-raising, and educational needs. For details, contact:

Kharis Media LLC
Tel: +1 (331) 312-2376
support@kharispublishing.com
www.kharispublishing.com

Andrea, I love you! Thank you for always standing by my side and encouraging me to follow the lord. Tripp and Andrew, I love you both! Thank you for being amazing sons! Always allow God's word and Spirit to do all that is necessary in your lives! After all, it is life.

Thank you to Rev. Daniel Taylor for your impact on my life and the lives of so many like me. You have left a legacy and shown us the way we are to walk.

Thank you to all of you truth seekers. You who truly desire to adhere and abide by the word of God. I pray this book will fill in the gaps and help you understand, to the fullness, of God's word.

CONTENTS

FOREWORD

It was my privilege to be one of Thomas Hammond, Jr.'s instructors while he was in college at Ozark Bible Institute in Neosho, MO. It is now my privilege to write this foreword for his book, *To The Children of Light.*

To say that it is important for Christians to be reminded that they are "Children of Light" is an understatement.

The Apostle John said that "men loved darkness rather than light, because their deeds are evil" (John 3:19). The Apostle Paul refers to Christians as "children of light" and admonishes us that we should "walk like children of light" (Eph. 5:8).

So, this book and the subject matter are definitely relevant to all true believers. Who cares what the *Ten Thunders of Revelation* said, "if you have not first a good grip on what it means "to be a Christian?"

So, my advice to the readers of this book is to look for ways that you may need to apply its lessons personally. Then, do as Nike says, "Just Do It!"

If we don't live right now, we won't get a chance to do it over after we die.

Selah – Think about it.

Rev. Daniel Taylor,

Pastor Emeritus/Instructor at OBI

INTRODUCTION

Albert Einstein once said, "Any fool can know. The point is to understand." This truth applies to Christians who know the Bible, but do not truly understand the fullness of all that is within its pages.

A fool hath no delight in understanding, but that his heart may discover itself (Proverbs 18:2).

We Christians often get into trouble with this. We know verses of scripture like John 3:16 or know stories like David and Goliath, but do not fully understand the depth and simplicity of how they apply to our lives. Instead, we like to pride ourselves on being able to spout scripture off to our own edification.

The church is a body. "For as we have many members in one body, and all members have not the same office:" (Romans 12:4 KJV). "So we, being many, are one body in Christ, and every one members one of another" (Romans 12:5 KJV).

The Body is not a denomination; it is not a creed; it's not even a building. What makes up the body of Christ are truly born-again, blood-bought people who have repented of sin and surrendered their lives to Christ. Why is it important to begin with this, because just like the human body, we know what is good for us but often neglect, forget, and ignore the very things that give us life, keep us going, and help us live productively full lives; or, in biblical terms, we neglect, set aside, forget, or ignore the very things that give us eternal life, help us continue steadfastly on this journey to heaven, and live fully productive, kingdom expanding lives!

In today's modern church, we see less teaching on biblical doctrines, less discipleship, minimal outreach, and a lack of understanding when it comes to biblical truths on leadership, church management, and, yes, even church discipline.

There is a lack of understanding concerning the ENTIRE Word of God. We have become "Ever learning, and never able to come to the knowledge of the truth." (1 Tim. 2:4).

My goal in writing this book is not to bash the Church; however, the purpose is found within the first few sentences of this introduction: to encourage the Christian and the church to have their eyes wide open, to fully understand what God says in His word, and to decidedly commit to following the contents within.

"He that hath my commandments, and keepeth them, he it is that loveth me: and he that loveth me shall be loved of my Father, and I will love him, and will manifest myself to him (John 14:21 KJV).

What promises from Christ? They're written in red, and we can take them to the bank. If we love Him, we will desire to honor Him by obeying His commandments. The rewarding result is that He will love us, the Father will love us, and Christ will reveal Himself deeper to us.

In this book, you might find several repeated references and thoughts. There is a reason for this:

I once preached a sermon at my church titled, "Beating a Dead Horse." It was a humorous title, but the purpose was to emphasize the need for repetition.

Bro. Taylor felt led to preach a message again that he had just preached that morning, stating, "The moment we start listening will be the moment that God will let me move on."

The Apostle Peter, in the book of 2 Peter, stated something similar. He was not concerned about whether people get tired of hearing the same thing repeatedly. It was necessary for them to be established in the truth!

He tells them in 2 Pet. 1:12, "Wherefore I will not be negligent to put you always in remembrance of these things, though ye know them, and be established in the present truth."

This is not a jab at their spiritual knowledge. This is not a casting of a shadow upon their salvation.

Peter takes upon himself personal responsibility—a responsibility given by God to keep the people of God grounded in doctrinal truth. Repetition of that doctrinal truth will keep the believer accountable and without excuse.

I pray that the Holy Ghost penetrates the hearts of every reader, that we are convicted of our half-hearted knowledge of the Bible, and that we fully become what God designed the church to be.

CHAPTER

1

ALL OR NOTHING

"All scripture is given by inspiration of God, and is profitable for doctrine, for reproof, for correction, for instruction in righteousness:"

(2 Timothy 3:16 KJV).

It's an early summer day, and a mother calls to her two sons to come to her room for daily devotions. Thirty minutes turned to an hour, and an hour turned to two of reading chapter after chapter, stopping only to explain the life application of what she had just read. That mother was my mother, and that was how I spent most all of my summer days and early school days. I remember moments in my parents' room or the living room, learning how the Bible applies to human life, the human condition, human thought, and the human heart.

I learned early on, as a child, that the Word of God is truly quick and powerful. The word of God is necessary for my spiritual growth and maturity. That the Word of God is life!

Billy Graham stated that, "One of the greatest needs of the church today is a return back to the scriptures as the basis of authority and to study them prayerfully in dependence on the Holy Spirit."

This quote so adequately sums up the greatest deficiency and necessity. My intention in this chapter is to cause our hearts and minds to become persuaded to make the Word of God, in its entirety, the foundation and the guide of our lives!

If we are not convinced of our need to adhere to all the Word of God, then we will do as others, while justifying ourselves. It's an attempt to adjust the Bible to our culture instead of the culture to the Word of God.

Now, the scripture that was referenced at the beginning is familiar, but not fully understood or followed. We like the inspiration, we like the profit, but we often overlook the FULL PURPOSE OF THE BIBLE!

I want to look at this verse and examine the purposes that the Bible serves.

The first word says so much! “ALL” is used for emphasis. It is the whole of one's energy and interest. Merriam-Webster’s Dictionary says “ALL” is the whole amount, quantity, or extent of. It is every member or individual component of. The whole number and sum of.

So, the scripture says that the whole of it, in every aspect, in its completeness, in its entirety, is inspired. (I hope you are getting the picture). Every word spoken by God, placed into the heart of man as the Holy Ghost moved upon them, spoken, and written down, is absolutely and unequivocally necessary for the biblical believer. “For the prophecy came not in old time by the will of man: but holy men of God spake as they were moved by the Holy Ghost (2 Peter 1:21 KJV).

Scripture was spoken by a Holy God, written down by Holy men, and anointed by the Holy Ghost. So, if the Word of God is Holy in every aspect of its origin and its current being, then we must be holy-minded to fully understand and receive the fullness of the Gospel.

But the natural man receiveth not the things of the Spirit of God: for they are foolishness unto him: neither can he know them, because they are spiritually discerned (1 Corinthians 2:14 KJV).

We cannot and will not understand what is Holy and godly if we walk after the flesh. We must walk in the fullness of the Spirit of God.

1 Corinthians 3:1 (KJV) — And I, brethren, could not speak unto you as unto spiritual, but as unto carnal, even as unto babes in Christ.

Paul, speaking to the church at Corinth, was dealing with those who were walking carnally. They understood some of the scripture, but on the level of a new convert, although they had been for some time apart in the church. They walked carnally and thus had a carnal view of the scriptures.

"They were still mere babes in Christ. They had received some of the first principles of Christianity, but had not grown up to maturity of understanding in them, or of faith and holiness…" (Matthew Henry Commentary).

It is of the utmost importance to us that we fully understand all that the scriptures say and not only understand but live by them.

James encourages us to let the Word of God be grafted into us, let it take hold and begin to produce fruit unto righteousness:

> Wherefore lay apart all filthiness and superfluity of naughtiness, and receive with

> meekness the engrafted word, which is able save your souls.
>
> But be ye doers of the word, and not hearers only, deceiving your own selves.
>
> or if any be a hearer of the word, and not a doer, he is like unto a man beholding his natural face in a glass (James 1: 21-23, KJV).

We must also understand the Bible's inspiration:

> The prophets and apostles did not speak from themselves, but what they received of the Lord that they delivered unto us. That the scripture was given by inspiration of God appears from the majesty of its style,-from the truth, purity, and sublimity, of the doctrines contained in it,-from the harmony of its several parts,-from its power and efficacy on the minds of multitudes that converse with it,-from the accomplishment of many prophecies relating to things beyond all human foresight,-and from the uncontrollable miracles that were wrought in proof of its divine original (Matthew Henry Commentary).

Every word, every period, every thought; is inspired by God through Divine revelation.

The Bible is profitable. Profit means to yield advantageous returns or results (Merriam-Webster

Dictionary). When we allow the Word of God to pierce our hearts, the results are out of this world. It is eternally beneficial for us. Its value is not measured by the world's system of value, for the Word of God does not have worldly origins; in fact, it is contrary to the world in every aspect. Its value is not monetary; its value is not worldly philosophy; its value is not human relationship, and yet, the Word of God encompasses all of life. "How so?" You may ask. Because, when God is at the center, when His word is abided by, then my marriage will be what is supposed to be; my relationship with my son will be what it is supposed to be; my relationship with other people will be what it is supposed to be; my finances will be the way they are supposed to be; and, my knowledge and wisdom will be what they are supposed to be; all with one thought driving it all...ETERNITY. The Bible's doctrines and principles cover and deal with every aspect of life and leave nothing unanswered.

Now, let us begin to look further into the scripture we began with. There are specific things that the Bible has profit in.

Doctrine: Doctrine is the belief or set of beliefs held and taught (Merriam-Webster Dictionary). The Word of God, when read personally, read from the pulpit, or in the Sunday school class, has value as a teacher. Its lessons are vast. It is in the Bible that we learn of the Power of God in Creation; it is in the Bible that we learn of the fall of man and the necessity of a redeemer; it is in the Bible that we learn lessons on obedience and sacrifice; and, it's where we learn the importance of being like Christ and exhibiting His characteristics.

Regardless of your denomination, there are specific beliefs held and taught.

Let us look at one of the highlights of Jesus' earthly ministry:

Matthew 5:

1. And seeing the multitudes, he went up into a mountain: and when he was set, his disciples came unto him:
2. And he opened his mouth, and taught them, saying,
3. Blessed are the poor in spirit: for theirs is the kingdom of heaven.
4. Blessed are they that mourn: for they shall be comforted.
5. Blessed are the meek: for they shall inherit the earth.
6. Blessed are they which do hunger and thirst after righteousness: for they shall be filled.

7. Blessed are the merciful: for they shall obtain mercy.
8. Blessed are the pure in heart: for they shall see God.
9. Blessed are the peacemakers: for they shall be called the children of God.
10. Blessed are they which are persecuted for righteousness' sake: for theirs is the kingdom of heaven.
11. Blessed are ye, when men shall revile you, and persecute you, and shall say all manner of evil against you falsely, for my sake.
12. Rejoice and be exceeding glad: for great is your reward in heaven: for so persecuted they the prophets which were before you. (KJV).

The people were willing to be taught. They wanted to hear from the Lord, and the Lord obliged them. The most successful students are those who understand the importance of willing ears and open hearts; for a lesson to truly have impact, it must be heard, received, and applied.

Christ begins with a blessing. Matthew Henry says a couple of things concerning this text:

> He came not only to purchase blessings for us, but to pour out and pronounce blessings on

> us; and here he does it as one having authority, as one that can command the blessing, even life for evermore, and that is the blessing here again and again promised to the good; his pronouncing them happy makes them so; for those whom he blesses, are blessed indeed.

Christ pronounces, with authority, and produces blessings upon His people.

Matthew continues:

> Each of the blessings Christ here pronounces has a double intention: I. To show who they are that are to be accounted genuinely happy, and what their characters are. II. What that is wherein true happiness consists, in the promises made to persons of certain characters, the performance of which will make them happy.

He shows the contrasting differences between the effects of this world and sin, with what awaits those who are saved and His. The physical action of the child of God will result in a spiritual reaction.

1. If you are poor in spirit, as a child of God, you will receive all the riches of heaven. Meaning, if you are emptied of all self, you have given all for Christ, your destination will be heaven.

> This self-emptying conviction, that 'before God we are void of everything,' lies at the foundation of all spiritual excellence, according to the teaching of Scripture. Without it we are inaccessible to the riches of Christ. [Jamieson, Fausset, and Brown (J, F, & B) Commentary.]

The poor in spirit understand that they are separated from God, but, because of that realization, they pursue the very thing that will repair the bridge that will bring them into right standing with God.

2. If you mourn, you will be blessed with the comfort that only God can provide. This second lesson is connected to the first. When we realize our need, there should arise within us a deep sorrow. When we realize our great deficiency, there comes a grievous mourning. We realize that there is nothing we can do to help ourselves. However, when this happens, we are shown One who can, and He comforts us by letting us know that we can be forgiven. This is shown in Isaiah chapter 6:1-5. Isaiah is presented with his own deficiency, and his response is one of great sorrow. J, F, & B states it this way:

It is poverty of spirit that says, "I am undone"; and it is the mourning which this causes that makes it break forth in the form of a lamentation. "Woe is me! for I am undone." Hence this class are termed "mourners in Zion," or, as we might express it, religious mourners, in sharp contrast with all other sorts (Isa 61:1-3 66:2).

3. Our spiritual poverty can end even now. How so? By our repentance of sin and our complete surrender to God. One day, our sorrow will be completely ended, God will wipe our tears from our eyes, and we will live in perpetual joy as we lay our eyes upon our Savior. We will no longer remember our trials or sorrows, for we will live eternally in the beauty and power of God's glory!

4. With this change that comes from God comes His character traits. Meekness is what Christ exhibited. Now, do not be confused. He was not weak, He was not a pushover, and He was not bashful. However, He was submissive. Not to man, but to His Father! As Christians, we are called to be submissive to God the Father. We are called to do His will, at His bidding. Meekness is power under restraint, submitting to a higher authority. Just as with the others, this comes with a blessing and a

promise. The meek's inheritance will be the earth. "The meek the only rightful occupants of a foot of ground or a crust of bread here, and heirs of all coming things." (J, F, &B Commentary).

5. "Blessed are they which hunger and thirst" (Matt. 5: 8). The Bible tells us right off that this is not a physical hunger or thirst, but one of a spiritual nature. The Bible says that they are blessed who hunger and thirst after righteousness. What is righteousness? Righteousness is "the quality or state of being morally correct and justifiable" (Oxford Dictionary).

So, blessed are the morally correct and justifiable before God. We are blessed when we truly seek to do what is godly and biblical. When we pursue Christ, we have the promise that we will be filled. We will not lack anything when we fully desire the things of God!

6. Have you ever been wronged by someone, and you could justifiably punish them for their wrongdoing, and yet you decide not to do anything but forgive them instead? Well, if you have, then you are blessed. The Bible tells us that when we show mercy, mercy will be shown to us. Becoming Christians, mercy was

shown to us by Christ's being sacrificed on the cross. So, because He showed great mercy to us, who did not deserve it, we should in turn show mercy.

7. "Blessed are the pure in heart" (Matt. 5: 8). Not only is this referring to those who have separated themselves from all things worldly, which would defile a person's heart, but also to those having a conscience clear before God. The promise is that we will see God, but a Holy and Pure God can only be visible to a holy and pure person. Christ, as our example, showed us that we could live in this world and yet remain pure in heart, mind, and body. If we ever expect to see God in all His glory, purity must be a part of who we are. We must separate ourselves, in all aspects, from anything that would defile us and keep us from seeing God.

8. I was listening to the radio, and the commentator mentioned this portion of scripture and said something very profound. We are called to be peace*makers* before we are called to be peace*keepers.* A peacemaker is someone who goes into a situation, whether spiritual or physical, that is complete chaos and disorder, and by the help of God working through them, brings about peace. A

peacekeeper is one who goes into a place that has already had peace and maintains that peace.

Now, although both have their importance, the bible blesses the peacemakers and gives us the promise: If we are these, we will be called the children of God. This puts quite a bit of responsibility upon the Christian. As children of God, we should foster peace. We should be the initiators of peace. When we walk into a situation where there is discord, peace should enter with us. Now, do not misunderstand. It has nothing to do with us, but because of Who is residing in us.

9. The last three verses are all coupled together. If you have heard me preach or read my other book, then you know that I strongly believe that we are not greater than our Lord. The Bible promises that we will be hated, mocked, persecuted, and even killed for our stand for Christ. However, with this also comes a blessing and a promise. When we truly stand for God and biblical truth, we will see and live in the Kingdom of God. — "He that findeth his life shall lose it: and he that loseth his life for my sake shall find it" (Matthew 10:39, KJV). We are encouraged to rejoice when we are persecuted and lied about, because we have the knowledge that we have been chosen

to suffer for Christ's sake, and we will see Him one day!

In 1 Timothy 4:16, we are told the importance of adhering to *all* doctrine: "Take heed unto thyself, and unto the doctrine; continue in them: for in doing this thou shalt both save thyself, and them that hear thee" (KJV).

Doctrine is a safety net when held and taught. My pastor, Rev. Jerry Smith, said, "We have a responsibility with what we know." Let us boldly tell others of what God's word says, so that not only are we saved, but they also have the chance to be as well.

There are several portions of scripture that share doctrinal truths. Statements of doctrines, such as the Assembly of God's 16 Fundamental Truths, are important tools to know what the Word of God says. I encourage you to find out what they are and study them. Know what you believe, why you believe it, and how to properly share the doctrines of the Bible with the world around you!

REPROOF is to rebuke. It is the criticism of a fault. It refers to an expression of blame and disapproval. God`s word reveals to us our faults. It rebukes us to bring about recognition of wrongdoing. Another word we are more familiar with, but have a challenging time receiving, is conviction. Yes, that is right!

CONVICTION: Conviction or reproof happens when God, by the Holy Ghost, puts His finger on something in our lives that should not be. Now I want us to fully understand that conviction is not bad! It is the complete opposite. Conviction is refining, causing us to be aware of the sin within our lives that must be addressed.

My sons would not know what was wrong unless reproof was used. We would not have known what was wrong without the Law of God, showing us our sin.

"And when he is come, he will **reprove** the world of sin, and of righteousness, and of judgment" (John 16:8).

Correction and Reproof are similar in their meanings and the consequences of not hearing and heeding their lessons.

CORRECTION: Correction is the action or process of correcting, setting a wrong right.

When Adam and Eve disobeyed God in the Garden of Eden, God brought correction. Punishment had to be handed out. However, the design of God was to provide a means to redeem (buy back) His creation.

If you read Genesis Chapter 3, then you will see three separate punishments handed out:

1. To the serpent: He would crawl on his belly, having the dust of the earth always in his face, and there would be friction forever between men and himself. This signified his end and prophesied what Jesus Christ the Lord would do to him.

2. To the woman: She would experience pain in childbirth and rearing. Sorrows would be multiplied. This means, as one sorrow ends, another one begins.

3. To the man: The ground would be cursed. He would have to sweat to get his food. He would have to remove rocks, stumps, and thorns to bring up something profitable to eat.

This correction was laid out justly. Man disobeyed, and God rightly set things right again. However, He knew men would never be able to set things right on their own. There had to be a sacrifice made. However, man's feeble attempts at sacrifices would still not be enough.

Hebrews 10:

1. For the law having a shadow of good things to come, and not the very image of the things, can never with those sacrifices which they

offered year by year continually make the comers thereunto perfect.

2. For then would they not have ceased to be offered? Because that the worshippers once purged should have had no more conscience of sins.

3. But in those sacrifices there is a remembrance again made of sins every year.

4. For it is not possible that the blood of bulls and of goats should take away sins.

So, we come to the greatest event that ever occurred for the better of humanity. The giving of Jesus Christ's life as the supreme and final sacrifice, planned from before the foundations of the world. We deserved the correction, but He did not. However, God, knowing there was no other way, provided the corrective measures needed to fully correct what man had undone.

"By the which will we are sanctified through the offering of the body of Jesus Christ once for all" (Hebrews 10:10).

Instruction in righteousness: The purpose of the Law, of the Bible, is to instruct a people, who are altogether ignorant of what is right. If we want to know what is pure, holy, and true, we will investigate the Word of God. We want wisdom, so we go to the

Word of God. In fact, this chapter, even this book, is for the purpose of instructing the saints of God and the sinner of what is right.

The necessity of choosing to adhere to "all of the counsel of God" is because every area of your life and how you handle things that arise will be markedly different. Your mind, marriage, children, ministry, etc., will be affected when you, as an individual, understand the Word of God's power, when surrendered to it.

As we go on throughout the book, please look at it prayerfully and with a desire to know and be taught what God has to say to His people. Even if the lesson reproves or corrects you, willingly submit to it and be made more like Christ.

CHAPTER

2

MISSED AND MISHANDLED

On May 8th, 2022, I became the Pastor of Faith Assembly of God, a town in Southeast Texas, my hometown. It was in those months prior and has been in the years that have followed, where God stirred my soul to prepare His church to be the church He had designed. The message I began to preach and to strongly push was one of the necessity of Biblical Christianity.

I remember sitting across from my uncle, and he asked me what I thought that meant. "What does biblical Christianity mean to you?" I thought carefully and proceeded to answer:

Biblical Christianity is the understanding that every area of my life, spirit, thought, etc., resides within the confines of God's Word. If God's Word declares that

I should do something, then I do it. If God's Word tells me not to do something, then I do not do it. It is not to assume God means something different, but to become a student of the entirety of the Word of God and willingly apply all of it to my life, through the Power of the Holy Ghost.

I believe my answer is what my uncle was looking for.

Biblical Christianity is not a new thought. It truly is simply living by God's Word.

"Simplicity of the Gospel," I have heard this phrase most of my adult life, as I am sure most of you have. However, I was met with the reality of what that means and looks like. We were doing a three-night kids crusade at a church that we have fellowship with, and in that crusade, an adult came under conviction, repented of his sins, and gave his life to Christ. Now, the message preached in the kids crusade was biblical truth, and yet it wasn't laced in a bunch of theological terminology; it didn't have original Greek and Hebrew words and meanings, and it wasn't introducing some great oracle speaker. It was simple, it was plain, it was straightforward, yet it was eternally impactful!

At this juncture, I feel it necessary to bring some explanation.

Preaching isn't hollering and spitting. Nothing is wrong with those things, for the preaching of the gospel stirs emotion, excitement, and urgency; but preaching is the proclamation of divine truth with urgency and conviction.

Teaching takes time to explain divine truth. It reveals, in a slow and intentional way, the mysteries of God. It is like the fertilizer placed in the garden. The seed has started growing, fertilization causes enhanced growth. It equips and arms the believer to have Christ in them and themselves in Christ.

So, the big question that may have been formulated in your mind with the few paragraphs that began this chapter is, "What does Biblical Christianity and the Simplicity of the Gospel have to do with the chapter topic?"

Simply this, the Western church world has missed and mishandled the Word of God to the detriment of the many souls that it has influenced worldwide. Many will find themselves eternally separated from God because they refused to adhere their lives to the Word of God.

Bible reading is devotional. The Word of God is the bread of life for the believer. It nourishes us daily.

The problem is this is like drinking milk. Bible study goes deeper. It is investigative. This is not coming up with your own truth but coming to understand THE TRUTH.

Bible reading and bible study is not just a pleasant idea and a box to check off. It is biblically mandated (Joshua 1:8, 2 Timothy 2:15).

We need to understand and fully believe that the Word of God is life to the believer. God's Word declares that any alterations to the infallible bring with them a certain fallibility:

> Every word of God is pure: he is a shield unto them that put their trust in him" (Pro 30:5).
>
> Add thou not unto his words, lest he reprove thee, and thou be found a liar (Pro 30:6).

Solomon is teaching his son, concerning the Word of God, two things:

1. It is pure: Clarke's Commentary on this section of the verse reveals to us a certain truth concerning God's word,

> Everything God has pronounced, every inspiration which the prophets have received, is pure, without a mixture of error, without dross. Whatever trials it may be exposed to, it is always like gold: it bears the fire, and comes out with the same luster, the same purity, and the same weight.

The purity of God's Word is a shield of protection to those who trust in it. How so? When the enemy lies, we know God's truth, and that truth protects us. When the world says it doesn't matter, we know God's truth!

2. It is not to be added to: The truth is this. God's Word needs nothing added. It needs no human improvement. To do so would not only undo the above point but also add to us the rebuke of God and the public display of our lie. We will lose all trustworthiness.

I am firmly persuaded that the church world has overwhelmingly been found lacking in true biblical understanding and application. Now, the result is a church world that is "ever learning, but never able to come to the knowledge of the truth" (2 Tim. 3:7).

Interpretation is the careful discerning of the original meaning – looking deeply into what God was saying to the people during that time. To do this we must look at the cultural setting and background, was it to an entire nation like the nation of Israel or select group of people like to one of the churches Paul wrote to, and what were the issues being dealt with?

This deep examination will naturally lead to; how can we, in modern times, apply it to our own lives, nation, and churches?

Application is important. It is living the truth that has been revealed by the Holy Spirit. The intention of the

Word of God is to reshape our decisions, relationships, and our worldview.

So, what must happen for the tide to be turned?

As the Word of God is the "true" church's standard and authority, let us examine the Bible's solution for such erroneous errors as missing and mishandling.

> For when for the time ye ought to be teachers, ye have need that one teach you again which be the first principles of the oracles of God; and are become such as have need of milk, and not of strong meat (Heb 5:12) .

What the writer of Hebrews is telling us is pretty straightforward. Hebrews' readers required the basics once again. They had been "in it" long enough to be teachers of the oracles of God, but they had not grown or matured and were now in need of something nourishing to stir up a desire for growth.

This chapter is meant to re-establish the necessity of Biblical truths and create a solid Biblical foundation.

The church must revisit those things that have been missed and mishandled; those things which have been overlooked, perhaps by those who thought they already knew everything concerning Christianity and the Bible; and those things which have been mishandled due to a lack of understanding of what God was really saying.

There is a doctrine taught throughout all of Scripture that has been both missed and mishandled in this modern church age.

The Doctrine of the Depravity of Man: This one for me was a hard pill to swallow. Why? Well, you see, I was raised in church. I was taught the stories. I knew the books of the Bible. I even participated in Bible quiz games at the youth camp. I raised my hands, cried, and behaved accordingly. However, I thought of myself more highly than I should have.

The church world is often trying to boost us in our own eyes by stating things like, "Since we are made in God's image, then we are in essence little gods."

This misses the very reality that, without God, you and I are nothing.

It wasn't until I was in my twenties and thirties that I was faced with this reality. My first contact with this Doctrine when it was made real to me was when I read Isaiah 6:

1. In the year that king Uzziah died I saw also the Lord sitting upon a throne, high and lifted up, and his train filled the temple.

2. Above it stood the seraphims: each one had six wings; with twain he covered his face, and with twain he covered his feet, and with twain he did fly.

3. And one cried unto another, and said, Holy, holy, holy, is the LORD of hosts: the whole earth is full of his glory.

4. And the posts of the door moved at the voice of him that cried, and the house was filled with smoke.

5. Then said I, Woe is me! For I am undone; because I am a man of unclean lips, and I dwell in the midst of a people of unclean lips: for mine eyes have seen the King, the LORD of hosts.

6. Then flew one of the seraphims unto me, having a live coal in his hand, which he had taken with the tongs from off the altar:

7. And he laid it upon my mouth, and said, Lo, this hath touched thy lips; and thine iniquity is taken away, and thy sin purged.

It was while reading this account that I realized that no matter my upbringing, no matter my position, no matter my talents, in the presence of the Holy and Righteous God, I was *undone*!

I further read in the books of Psalms that God must humble Himself to even look upon me (Psalm 113:6). I was in shock, the Almighty gazes upon me and must humble Himself to do so!

Understand, it is not because He is prideful. God transcends all. The high and lofty places, of which we place such great importance, cannot compare. He is far beyond so that we could never reach Him. Yet, He came down. The great humility is when Jesus, through Kenosis. Kenosis refers to Christ's voluntary renunciation—not of His divine nature, but of the independent use of His divine attributes. This concept is found in Philippians 2:7, where it says Christ "emptied Himself, taking on the form of a servant.

I am a wretch. I am a worm. I am nothing but dust and yet the Almighty looks upon me! I am overwhelmed, and I cry out as Isaiah, "Woe is me! For I am undone!"

The truth behind this Doctrine is this: when we recognize who we are in light of the Word of God, we begin to fully see and understand who God is and what He desires to do in our lives.

Our response to His glory, to His call, will determine if we are transformed by God or whether we stay in our self-righteous state.

Another Doctrine I believe has been mishandled and missed is that of Conversion.

> Repent ye therefore, and be converted, that your sins may be blotted out, when the times

of refreshing shall come from the presence of the Lord (Acts 3:19 KJV).

We must understand that the "come as you are and stay as you are" mentality of modern Christianity is absolutely contrary to the Word of God and a detriment to the soul of every person who is taught it.

One of the most used statements spouted by most people when they don't see the need to change for Christ is, "He sees my heart." Equally, people with this mentality say, "The Bible says to work out my salvation on my own."

These mentalities are dangerous. Why? Because they remove the authority of God's mandate to be converted.

The heart, the Bible tells us, is desperately wicked. The heart is deceitful above all things, and desperately wicked: who can know it? (Jeremiah 17:9 KJV). The heart must be made new. We are incapable of changing our hearts on our own: "A new heart also will I give you, and a new spirit will I put within you: and I will take away the stony heart out of your flesh, and I will give you a heart of flesh" (Ezekiel 36:26).

We are incapable of saving ourselves; the latter end of Philippians 2:12-13 tells us two very important truths which are often overlooked in the truth of "Working out your own Salvation."

1. "With fear and trembling" – Not with presumption, not arrogantly, but with humility and holy reverence for the one who saves.

2. "It is God who works" – He is the force behind the transformation that takes place in the soul that is yielded to Him. It's of His pleasure that the work is started and completed.

Without mincing words, Paul instructs the Corinthians that, if someone is in Christ, he is made new. The person he was prior to salvation no longer exists! "Therefore if any man be in Christ, he is a new creature: old things are passed away; behold, all things are become new" (2 Corinthians 5:17 KJV).

I love watching new converts. They come, get saved, and immediately are eager to know more! I remember back in 2017 or 2018, a couple came in and were radically saved! Their testimony still causes excitement in my spirit.

However, what must be understood is this: they were *converted.* I'll let them tell you about their conversion experience in their own words.

From the woman, as written by her:

> If you only knew. If you only knew where I was before Christ, and where He brought me from. If you only knew what it took to get me to where I am now in the Lord. You wouldn't

question the way I want to live now. You wouldn't question why I dress the way I do. You wouldn't question why I don't watch the things I used to. Or why I do not listen to the same music as I did before. You wouldn't wonder why I don't continue to go and get the things I once thought was cool or meant something, put on my body. You wouldn't wonder why I don't hang around the same sin I used to. I can't and I won't. I will tell you I lost a lot of time with several people including my kids because of alcohol. Just to "have fun" in the moment. God changed me in January of 2016. I was delivered from alcohol. I drank every single day. I went clubbing during the week. It was an addiction for me. If He can do it for an alcoholic like me, He can do it for anyone!

I won't go back. You see, if I did, I'd die. Maybe not just physically, but more importantly, spiritually. God spared my life. He's given me hope. He's renewed my whole entire life. Am I perfect? No. Do I strive to do my very best though? Yes. He took the addictions and my sins, the endless pit I was in and brought me back to life. My life didn't end when I got saved. The things I once thought were, "fun" were no longer fun. However, the

> things of my life that were put on the back burner became life. God 1st of all, My children, My faith, and my love. I am no longer bound. God is the ONLY ONE who can pull you out. Not your mom, your dad, your grandparents, your kids, nobody. God is it. You've got to surrender. I almost didn't have a choice back in 2016. The devil almost had his way. God spared not only my life, but my husband's as well ONE...MORE...TIME.
>
> I could tell you my whole story of what happened that night in January of 2016, but you'd never believe me. So, take my word. The devil almost won... he almost had me! But, Jesus said, "this one is mine!" I don't feel as though I was worth it, but He said, "Yes you are!!!"
>
> He saved me that night in 2016, then filled me with the Holy Ghost in 2019. I am forever changed!

Looking into another doctrinal truth, we say, "Jesus is the Lord of my life." However, by the way many live today in the modern church; I am not convinced that we truly understand what that means, nor what it requires. I believe we have missed the deeper truth.

> That if thou shalt confess with thy mouth the Lord Jesus, and shalt believe in thine heart

that God hath raised Him from the dead, thou shalt be saved (ROMANS 10:9).

"You don't make Him Lord. He's Lord already. You just recognize it." –Adrian Rogers

That's what lordship is – Christ reigning as supreme authority over our life. Making Jesus Lord of our life is not something passive. It's not a state of being; it's a state of doing. Those whom Jesus recognizes as His own are those who do the will of His Father in heaven – Keith Green.

Christ's lordship is a blessed hope for some & a terrifying nightmare for others. Regardless of our response, it is an unalterable reality –Paul Washer.

What do you think of when you hear the word Lord or Lordship?

Lordship means Sovereignty, Supreme Power, Authority, Dominion.

For the Christian, it means that we have surrendered our lives, will, emotions, and spirit to His guidance and power.

It means we yield to His higher ways and understanding.

It means we trust that He will, since we belong to Him, protect and provide the necessities of our physical, and even more importantly, our spiritual needs.

It means we submit to His mastery over us. However, do not misunderstand. His Lordship is not despotism. It is not, because we must willingly become subject to Him.

Why should we do this?

We do this, by the Spirit of God revealing it to us, because we understand that within us is nothing good; we understand that without Him there is no hope or life only death and destruction, and we understand that due to the sacrifice of the Son on the cross that He deserves nothing less than our complete allegiance.

What makes Christ Lord?

His hand in creation. He was the word spoken that initiated the heavens coming to be and the earth being formed.

He was prophesied of by the elders and prophets of old. He was born miraculously into this world, forever changing the course of man's destiny, if man will but choose Him over all others. He walked among us as Emanuel, healing and calling all who will to come to Him and be saved! He willingly laid His life down as the final and Supreme sacrifice to bridge the gap between God and man. He rose again to solidify our eternal hope of life with Him. He sits at the right hand of God the Father, ever making intercession for us. He is Jesus Christ the Lord! There is none like Him, and on the day, when all will stand before Him, then all will bow down and confess that Jesus Christ is Lord.

Paul shows us three things in Romans 10:9.

I. We must confess with our mouths.

What must we confess? That Jesus is Lord. We must recognize His Lordship over our lives and submit willingly to Him. We must confess that without Him, we are undone, weak, and incapable of helping ourselves outside of His divine care. It must be ever in our minds and always on our mouths that Jesus Christ is LORD!

II. We must believe in our hearts.

We must treasure and hold to the entirety of God's word! We must love it and believe it with every fiber of our being. We must hold to the truth written that our Savior is risen!

III. We will be saved.

This promise will come to those who do the above. We will be saved. We will be saved from the wrath of

God the Father and Jesus Christ that will be poured out on all who sin! We will be saved from eternal punishment and separation due to sin. We will be saved from agony and sorrow. We will forevermore be where there is only peace and joy.

CHAPTER

3

A LETTER TO THE CHURCH OF JESUS CHRIST

"…upon this rock I will build my church; and the gates of hell shall not prevail against it"

(Matthew 16:18 KJV).

This is truly one of my favorite texts found in the Word of God.

There are certain parts of scripture that I have personally termed "Great declarations".

One such 'Great declarations' is found in Roman's 8:38, where Paul states, "I am persuaded…"

Paul was declaring His certainty. He had experienced Christ. He had experienced His love and forgiveness. He had experienced His provision and empowerment.

There would be nothing that could sway His devotion to Christ.

Let's define the word "church." Actually, the definition can best be found in 1 Corinthians 12. I'll give you a hint while you go and read that chapter—it involves you and me.

If you just can't wait, I'll tell you now. The Body, the members, those saved by Christ, are the church. Yes, that's right, some of the very ones we rub elbows with, and we do not always get along with. The church is made up of you and me, who are redeemed by the blood of Christ.

The verse mentioned above, Matthew 16:18, is the Lord's response to one of those declarations.

Let's take a look at it.

> Mat 16:13 When Jesus came into the coasts of Caesarea Philippi, he asked his disciples, saying, Whom do men say that I the Son of man am?
>
> Mat 16:14 And they said, Some say that thou art John the Baptist: some, Elias; and others, Jeremias, or one of the prophets.
>
> Mat 16:15 He saith unto them, But whom say ye that I am?
>
> Mat 16:16 And Simon Peter answered and said, Thou art the Christ, the Son of the living God.

> Mat 16:17 And Jesus answered and said unto him, Blessed art thou, Simon Barjona: for flesh and blood hath not revealed it unto thee, but my Father which is in heaven.

> Mat 16:18 And I say also unto thee, That thou art Peter, and upon this rock I will build my church; and the gates of hell shall not prevail against it.

I want to first make us aware that Christ wasn't telling Peter that the church would be built on Peter's shoulders. What was being stated was, the confession Peter had made of Jesus being the Son of God is what Christ would build His church upon.

This knowledge of the Second Person of the Holy Triune Godhead was indeed the very Son of God. That God was made flesh and dwelt amongst us! Peter, on his own, would not be able to live up to the holy perfection required to have a living, breathing, active body thrive upon him. No, it must be the perfect, spotless, holy Lamb of God!

Christ Jesus alone could cause such an army to rise up and turn the world upside down, without even raising a sword or spear! He alone could work in and through generations of men and women who had, as Peter did, confessed that Jesus Christ is the Son of the Living God! Upon this, this confession of faith and acknowledgement that Christ is the Son of God, is what the Church, you and I are built upon.

For the Church to be the Church, it must remember what it was founded upon! This is the letter to the Church, and much like the churches in Revelation, there has been a call made--we must "do again the first works."

The necessity of getting back to the Bible must permeate every fiber of the Church's being! It must be constantly at the forefront of the Church's mind! We must understand we are founded upon the Living Christ, the Son of the Living God!

The Church must be the Church! We must get out of the way, take our hands off of it, remove our ideals, stop quenching the Spirit, and let the Church be the Church!

I'm not anti-programs and outreach; however, what I am against is a church trying to move, work, and reach out without being led by the Word of God through the Spirit of God.

Now, back to the Church. Who are they who make the Church? How do we know that they are really the Church? Even more seriously, how do we know we are a part of the Church?

The Bible tells us that we will know them by their fruits: "Wherefore by their fruits ye shall know them" (Matthew 7:20 KJV). I know this verse is referring to false prophets, but the same can be said of the Church!

How can we know if the Church is the Church? How can we know it is true and settled with sound doctrine?

1. Is the fullness of the Word of God preached?

   Do we allow the word of God to be preached to its fullest, even if it makes us uncomfortable, even if it seems long, even if it seems not to apply to us, even if we've heard it before?

Do we hinder the word of God from being able to take root in our hearts?

Do we hinder the word of God from breaking up the fallow ground?

Do we hinder the word of God from breathing life into us or into someone around us?

The danger of not allowing the fullness of God's Word to have its perfect work individually and corporately is the effect on us and those around us when we do not.

Our facial expressions speak louder than our words! If we feel disinterested and disingenuous about the Word of God, others will see that, and it could rub off on them!

The truth is this, you and I will be held accountable for what we do with this Word! It doesn't matter our pedigree or how long we have been in this Christian life; we will give an account.

The following verse, which has already been referred to, applies to each of us, and it should be refreshed in our mind the purpose of the Word of God and the preaching of that Word!

"All scripture is given by inspiration of God, and is profitable for doctrine, for reproof, for correction, for instruction in righteousness" (2 Tim. 3:16).

2. Is the Spirit of God able to move freely and work freely as He sees fit?

The Bible tells us, with four words, a very profound and stern command! "Quench not the Spirit" (1Thess 5:19).

Why? Because it is by the Spirit of God that conviction comes, and we can know what must be changed within our hearts!

It is also because, by the Spirit of God that a conviction and drawing of the sinner occurs.

It is by the Spirit of God that the broken, captive, hurt, sick, demon-possessed and oppressed, fearful, and spiritually defeated lives get turned around!

Let us not dare quench the Spirit of God, for we know not for whom He is present to help and save!

Those of the true Church of God, the true Bride of Christ, will have a deep desire for Him to have His perfect way in their midst. The true Church wouldn't dare to disparage Him.

3. Does our love for one another betray us to those around us that we are His disciples?

   John 13:34 A new commandment I give unto you, That ye love one another; as I have loved you, that ye also love one another.

   John 13:35 By this shall all men know that ye are my disciples, if ye have love one to another.

Christ loved us so much, He gave Himself for us! He didn't show that love through gossiping and backbiting. He didn't show this love, demanding anything in return. He didn't show this love by stirring up strife, no, in fact, He encouraged us to love one another because it mattered to our testimony of Him! Of what He represents! Of What His purpose was!

He represented God the Father, and we represent God the Son! What does our testimony say about us?

4. Do we give more time to the things of God?

   No man can serve two masters: for either he will hate the one, and love the other; or else he

> will hold to the one, and despise the other. Ye cannot serve God and mammon (Matt. 6:24).
>
> No servant can serve two masters: for either he will hate the one, and love the other; or else he will hold to the one, and despise the other. Ye cannot serve God and mammon (Luke 16:13).

If we put events, sports, vacations, and work before God, then we have put God to the back burner of our hearts and have declared other things more important than He! It will only become easier to neglect the things of God!

Of course, a great danger would be this: "What one generation does in moderation, the next will do in excess" (unknown).

5. Do we give worship in the form of tithes and offerings as commanded by Scripture?

   I have purposely changed my wording. The reality of giving is this: It's an act of worship.

   What we give, no matter our opinions on tithing or giving, should be understood as the act of worship it is!

   He is worthy of our best. He is worthy of more than we could ever give, yet that understanding should never cause us not to try our best to give our best!

So, let us ask some examining questions:

- Do we give the Lord what He has asked for?
- Do we give with a willing and rejoicing heart?
- Do we view giving as an act of worship?

The reality is, anything we have was given by the Lord. He has blessed us abundantly and should be recompensed for the little He has asked of us, plus so much more!

6. Are we faithful in all things concerning God and our testimony of Him?

Faithfulness to God's house, prayer meeting, and Sunday school tells others and God that He is our priority! That He matters more than anything else in this world! It tells others that because of our deep Love for God, we will be devoted to Him, despite what non-essential things go on around us!

Many have opted to put other things before the Lord. What must be understood is that anything that takes God's place in our lives as a supreme priority is idolatry.

We must be cautious not to allow ourselves or things to become idols before God.

7. Do we lay aside every weight and sin?

"Ye did run well; who did hinder you that ye should not obey the truth?" (Gal 5:7).

We have traded the truth for this phrase: "Well, God hasn't personally convicted me of it." I believe in "personal convictions," but labeling things as such has been used as a crutch for those who don't want to lay aside the very things that will keep them out of hell!

The Bible, God's Word, is a black and white kind of book. It doesn't take some great, smart theologian to understand what "thou shalt not," "don't do it," and "abstain from" mean!

Be careful of using the phrase, "God knows my heart." Yes, He does know. He is absolutely aware. If there is any rebelliousness, any sin, or any weight in us, He will certainly know and deal with it accordingly.

8. Are we willing to die for the cause of Christ?

   To die, whether by the crucifying of our fleshly lusts, or by the actual laying down of our lives because we love the Lord enough to stand even if others fall?

   One of my all-time favorite books and one that I regularly recommend is "Foxe's Book of Martyrs".

   I would challenge you, read this book. See the spiritual fortitude that must be had to say boldly, "

Do what you will, I will not turn my back on my Savior."

9. Are we willing to take discipline with a heart right attitude that says, "Perhaps I need to seek the Lord about this, and if it's true, let Him change me."

My mother and I were talking once, like we often do, along with some others, and we got on the topic of church discipline.

I made this statement and it shook me, "If church discipline were carried out the way it was in the early church, we would lose half of our church."

We must understand that if the preacher preaches something from the Word of God that just so happens to plow our row, it is not because the pastor has been reading your mail, text messages, Facebook posts, etc. It is because He has labored before the face of God, and God dealt with Him directly in a way that burdened Him down to conviction! It often comes with a wish to preach something different, but he cannot escape what God has burdened him with and knows He must speak and sound the trumpet, because, as the watchman, He will be held accountable for what He did with the knowledge provided to Him!

We will dive into church discipline in more detail later on in this book, but please consider now the importance of this detail that God ordained for His church.

10. Do we actively reach for the lost, weep for the lost, and preach to the lost as we equally look for Christ to return?

    I remember being in college and God stirring me specifically about my praying for a burden and a vision for the lost.

    He said a couple of things to me that I have never forgotten!

    "Stop praying for a burden, if you won't tarry long enough for Me to give it to you."

    "Praying for a vision will not help if you constantly fill your eyes with lusts of this world."

We are called to be a light in darkness; however, I believe most Christians have two processes of thought. Neither of them is biblical.

1. Me-myself-and-I Attitude

   My pastor, the late Rev. Jerry Smith, told our church one service. "We cannot reap the harvest if we are constantly being the harvest." The reality is this: We come to church to get ourselves fixed, but we're in a spiritual rut. We slide right back in it and come the next service to do the whole process over again. We, the Church, have found ourselves very comfortable doing this. Meanwhile, there are souls who need us to get our heads on straight, stop looking inward only, and start looking, reaching, and going outward.

2. It's-not-my-ministry Attitude

   We view soul-winning solely as the responsibility of others or the pastor. We will work if we are over a ministry, but we don't want to be what the Bible calls "helps". This mentality has led many churches to have the same people doing far more things than they are capable of doing, causing spiritual, mental, emotional, and physical fatigue. This results in ministries being dropped and efforts by those same faithful workers to become subpar.

We must change our mentality and approach to personal evangelism and corporate outreach.

The familiar scripture tells us, "And he said unto them, Go ye into all the world, and preach the gospel to every creature" (Mark 16:15 KJV).

A general during WW2 was a well-known, confessing Christian. When asked by a reporter how he interpreted the Great Commission, the general replied, "It's not something you interpret, it's something you do."

We all have a purpose in God's kingdom. We all are called to be "vessels, meet for the master's use."

We all must endeavor to have His eyes to see, His heart to feel, His hands to reach, and His feet to go. Those of the world are counting on us, even if they don't know it, to be a light in their darkness!

So, where do the above ten things leave us?

The fact is, even if we only do five out of ten, we are far from what the Word of God calls the Church. We must let the Church be the Church!

We must ask ourselves, "What is the Church?" and "Why is it so important?" Then, prayerfully read God's Word for the answer.

We must do some deep self and corporate examination and see if we have hindered the Work and Word of God! We must stop trying to mix up our fleshly minded and worldly-driven ideas with the things of God and God's Word!

We all want to make it to heaven; there is not one of us who has a desire that is opposite. However, we must be the proper representation of Christ! We must be the Church that He has called us to be! We must have the Power of God at work within us and through us. We must have the anointing of God!

In my humble opinion, the reason this is all necessary is that time is running out. God WILL NOT give the signal to rapture the church, if the church is less than what He left in the book of Acts!

Which brings us to another point of discussion. What is a Book-of-Acts church?

Let us, once again, examine God's Word for the answer.

> 42 And they continued steadfastly in the apostles' doctrine and fellowship, and in breaking of bread, and in prayers.
>
> 43 And fear came upon every soul: and many wonders and signs were done by the apostles.
>
> 44And all that believed were together, and had all things common;
>
> 45 And sold their possessions and goods, and parted them to all men, as every man had need.
>
> 46 And they, continuing daily with one accord in the temple, and breaking bread from house to house, did eat their meat with gladness and singleness of heart,

> 47 Praising God, and having favour with all the people. And the Lord added to the church daily such as should be saved (Acts 2:42-47).

To design means to create, fashion, execute, or construct according to plan; to have as a purpose; to devise for a specific purpose or end.

God has had a design, a plan, a specific blueprint with a definitive purpose and a specific end.

His design is as evident as the pages where His spoken words are written. He laid out a design in creation for the purpose of declaring who He is. He laid out a design for marriage and the family—one man and one woman, created for one another and to raise a family, to declare who He is. He laid out His design for the temple in the Old Testament—to be a dwelling place for His glory, to testify of who He is! Do you see the pattern? Everything God has done, even down to sending Christ to die for mankind and to bring about the first church, is for the distinct purpose of declaring who He is.

> By God's design, he has wired his children for spiritual reproduction. He has woven into the fabric of every single Christian's DNA a desire and ability to reproduce — David Platt.

This means that what God did for us must be shared with someone else, so that he too can be saved.

Our text has five things that break down God's design for His Church.

1. Connect – This focuses on the vertical and horizontal relationships in life. It begins with Salvation and continues through to building strong spiritual relationships with God and man. The vertical relationships focus on the process that connects people with God, on the horizontal focus on building relationships person to person.

    - Each fellowship with the other for the purpose of becoming united as one in Christ.

    - They prayed together often.

2. Grow – Grow is about discipleship. It's how what is spiritually grown within our lives and the lives of those we share the gospel with. Its focus is all about growing to become more like Christ!

"But grow in grace, and in the knowledge of our Lord and Saviour Jesus Christ. To him be glory both now and for ever. Amen." (2 Peter 3:18)

The early church did not stray away from the teachings of the Apostles, who received their teaching from Christ. We shouldn't stray either. For in His words is life!

When we are eager to learn the doctrines of Christ, we come to know what He desires in our lives. When we allow Him to make those changes in our lives, then we can be what He called us to be in someone else's life.

3. Serve – The Bible tells us that when we become children of God, we also become His priests to represent Him to everyone around us. Basically, we all serve a purpose in the Kingdom of God. We are all called to be priests for His glory!

"But ye are a chosen generation, a royal priesthood, an holy nation, a peculiar people; that ye should shew forth the praises of him who hath called you out of darkness into his marvellous light" (1 Peter 2:9 KJV).

4. Go – Evangelism. Reaching out to those who are next door and those across the globe. Your testimony is the key to opening the door for evangelism to happen. We are all given that command. We all must take it as part of our responsibility. It is not the job alone of the pastor or lay minister, but of every person called a child of God.

Those in the early church were…

- bold in living out their faith.
- careful to meet the needs of those around them, even those who were without a body.

- used in their bold testimony and evangelism so that souls were added daily, such as should be saved.

3. Worship – This is the intimacy and reality of the presence of Christ when we, as a church, are following God's design for the Church.

In worship, Christ is in our midst; we can see His power at work, and we can feel His power in our lives.

Worship is more than music and lyrics, although those are included; it is also prayer and Holy Ghost-anointed preaching.

My desire is for us to remember God's design, to truly know God's design, and to adhere to that design.

My desire is for the church to be empowered by the Holy Ghost to fulfill this design. We cannot do it with our intellect; we cannot do it with our good intentions; we must be empowered to be and do what God has called us to be and do.

We need to understand that if we only succeed in one area but fail to follow God's design in the others, then we are doing God, ourselves, and the world around us a disservice.

CHAPTER

4

BIBLICAL LEADERSHIP

"There is no such thing as a self-made spiritual leader. A true leader influences others spiritually only because the Spirit works in and through him to a greater degree than in those he leads"

– J. Oswald Sanders.

It had been so long in coming. A journey many never dreamed they would make. However, the excitement in the air was undeniable. They began to sing old yet familiar songs. The children began to dance and laugh in the streets. The king had declared them free to return to their homeland and to rebuild the dwelling place of their God. Not only encouraging them to build, but also providing materials to bring their desire to pass.

Do you know this story? Well, if it hasn't rung any bells yet, allow me to continue:

They rebuilt the cities that had once been destroyed. Old and young alike were wonderfully satisfied with the progress. They restored the practices of sacrifice and offerings. Old and young alike, in agreement, were satisfied.

Finally, came the day they all had been awaiting. The older pictured what they once knew so familiarly. The younger, who had no clue what to expect, were excited and full of desire. The rebuilding of the Tabernacle had begun.

At the laying of the foundation, rejoicing began, music began, and worship began. However, it was equally matched by weeping. What could cause such a sound that the inhabitants around them couldn't discern the difference?

The younger rejoiced at the great prospect of things that had never been seen before. The elders wept because they remembered what it once looked like.

There was a disconnect: The younger excited about the hope of the future; the elder, unable to escape the past.

Have you figured it out yet? If not, go read the book of Ezra, go ahead, I'll wait for you.

What is needed in the hour that we live is the older generation arising to a glorious opportunity to encourage the younger generation in their pursuit of all things truly biblical. To encourage them in the laying of the foundation of a real relationship with the God of their Fathers, the Great "I AM"!

"Servanthood Responsibility" is what comes to mind when I consider what being a biblical leader is. In my short years in ministry, I have determined to learn the best way to be a biblical leader, to take what God says about leaders, and to apply it to my life. I wanted to learn how to be a biblical leader to my wife, to my children, as a Christian in the church and the world, as a youth pastor, and now as a pastor.

Now, before we go any further, I need you to know: I write this chapter, not as one who has learned all that needs to be learned. I write this chapter, not as one who is a supreme example of biblical leadership. I write as someone who recognizes that I am no leader, much less a great leader, outside of Christ. Anything that I might be is only found in my surrender to Jesus.

As a school administrator, I hold daily staff devotions in the morning prior to the students' arrival. One morning, the lesson was on "The Servant's Heart." I explained that the greatest asset a worker/leader could have is a servant's heart. Such a heart is exhibited through work quality, attitude towards tasks, and how we treat one another.

This 'servant's heart' has its roots in humility, which is not weakness, but meekness.

I explained that we all have a higher authority to which we must answer. "You, as the staff, answer to me. Yet, we, as believers, answer to God."

When I consider the servant's heart of humility and meekness, I can't help but go to the Scriptures and take a glimpse into the heart of the One who exhibited the greatest forms of servanthood, humility, and meekness.

"Jesus knowing that the Father had given all things into his hands, and that he was come from God, and went to God" (John 13:3)

"He riseth from supper, and laid aside his garments; and took a towel, and girded himself" (John 13:4).

"After that he poureth water into a bason, and began to wash the disciples' feet, and to wipe them with the towel wherewith he was girded" (John 13:5).

This event, in my mind, is one of the greatest events to take place. Christ, knowing His position and power, determined within the last final hours of His life to teach His followers about servanthood. Imagine with me: The Disciples have been traveling in the dust, dirt, and mud. Christ, the Word, who was in the beginning, God made flesh, put on a servant's robe, grabbed a basin of water and a towel, knelt down in front of them, and washed their feet!

Paul, in declaring an essential truth for the Philippian church to understand, stated,

> Who, being in the form of God, thought it not robbery to be equal with God:
>
> But made himself of no reputation, and took upon him the form of a servant, and was made in the likeness of men:
>
> And being found in fashion as a man, he humbled himself, and became obedient unto death, even the death of the cross (Phip 2:6-8).

In all that Christ did, He never denied who He was and Who had sent Him, but He never became arrogant.

I want to address and bring our attention to an elephant in the room. Acts 6:3 and 1 Timothy 3 give the qualifications of an overseer and a deacon. Now, we can debate these, and in fact, there have been endless debates concerning the different aspects of these qualifications and what was meant. However, I want us to first understand that these qualifications are not something that these men had to attain, but were already possessors of. Second, these qualifications can be and should be attained. Our desire should be to be made more like Christ, not only as leaders, but as His followers. As Christ is constantly making us new and working a perfect work in us by the Spirit of God and the Word! Thirdly, unfortunately, in today's culture, you will be hard pressed to find anyone who matches these qualifications exactly. If they are the husband of one wife, yet they do not have control (ruleth) of their home, they do not qualify. If they control their home but they have had immoral addictions, they do not qualify. Looking on a woman to lust after her is committing adultery (Matthew 5:28). If they are exact on all the qualifications, but they are of a quick temper to fighting, they are not qualified.

My point is this, whatever your spiritual status, arise to the call to become a spiritual biblical leader!

As Christians, we do lead, whether it be as laity or as pastor, and all in-between. Allow me to write to you what Christ has shown me. (Understand that this is what Christ showed me personally, as a man, from His word. The principles laid out in scriptures, however, apply to all believers.)

First, as a husband: "For the husband is the head of the wife, even as Christ is the head of the church: and he is the saviour of the body" (Eph 5:23).

"But I would have you know, that the head of every man is Christ; and the head of the woman is the man; and the head of Christ is God" (1Co 11:3).

"Strong churches have strong families, and strong families have strong husbands and fathers."

This was the thought I had on a Sunday morning, while encouraging the men of my church. I remember the moment when I spoke it. I became convicted in my spirit.

Know that I am not talking about a dictatorship in your marriage. The wife is not a rug to wipe your feet on. We are given the responsibility to care for her gently, tenderly, lovingly, and sacrificially.

It is a domino effect: If we want to have strong, biblical churches. If we want our churches to be full of the Holy Ghost power, and if we want our churches to grow in the things of God. Then the corresponding action is that we have spiritually strong families! If ours are to be spiritually strong families, they must be biblical. We must have families that are full of the Holy Ghost and Power! We must have families that grow in the things of God! To have this, the men must rise and do what is required to see it come to pass!

It is a dynamic that is God ordained. It is a dynamic that is absolutely needed in a culture where the father is made out to look like an idiot and masculinity is viewed with great despise. It is a dynamic that begins with us men's surrender to Christ!

I. The Priest of our Home! – We are to show our families how to intercede in prayer by interceding on their behalf daily!

Men, there is a real devil, and he is out to destroy our families! He is out to bring death into our homes! He is out for you and me to stop being the defender of our Homes by causing us to believe that being biblical as fathers and husbands is not important!

If our Home has weak defenses, it is directly due to you and me, Men!

II. The Prophet of our Home! – We are to instruct our homes in the things of God! We must become proficient in understanding the Word of God, so we can instruct our homes in what God is declaring! When we can discern the voice of God from every other ungodly, foul voice out there, then we can better instruct our homes how to discern the voice of God!

The prophet of the Home will faithfully, willingly, and with authority instruct His household according to the Word of God!

III. The King of our Home! – In your mind right now, what is the purpose of a king? When I think of being the king of my Home, I think of three things.

1. The Authority – I must know my position in leading my Home. I lead my home as Christ leads me. I maintain spiritual order in my Home. I maintain discipline in my Home. I, with accountability to God and His Word, take responsibility for my family and my role in my home!

2. The Defender – I will fight hell for my family! I will go through fire for my family! I will do what is required to maintain the safety and protection of my family! My family will not have to wonder whether or not I would die for them; they know that answer by the way I live according to God's Word!

3. The Provider – The Bible says that if a man doesn't work, He doesn't eat. My family will be directly impacted by how I provide for them! My goal is not to give them what they want, necessarily, but it is my goal to provide for their necessities! In our culture today, men would rather be lazy than work!

Second, as a father:

> One that ruleth well his own house, having his children in subjection with all gravity;

> For if a man know not how to rule his own house, how shall he take care of the church of God? (1 Timothy 3:4).

You will read several times where I use the term, "Father/fatherhood." Understand that this is what I believe fathers should attain. However, don't believe for one second that anyone can easily apply these biblical truths.

"Biblical fatherhood calls for a different standard of leadership." I was doing some reading and came across this phrase. It struck me so deeply. I'm reminded of the song, "Lord, I want to be just like you, 'cause he wants to be just like me." The driving force of parenting should be summarized in that thought.

The best leaders are those who lead by example. As Christ led by example, so should we as parents strive to lead by the same example left to us by our heavenly Father in the life of Christ.

The last series that I, as a youth pastor, did was a series with the young people on "God's Biblical Design". We covered a wide variety of areas, but I specifically covered, with the young men, what it means to be a biblical man. Being biblical, as a refresher, means "of, relating to, or being in accord with the Bible."

In a culture where being a godly, masculine man is frowned upon, it is the responsibility of the men of God to become influential in the lives of young men, training them to become men of God.

The great missionary, the Apostle Paul, showed us what it looked like to have a biblical father/son relationship. I want to look at some specific things concerning the scripture from which we read.

1. The Father and Son relationship between Paul and Timothy

Paul had taken Timothy under His wings, so to speak. If we read in the beginning of this book, Paul writes in1 Tim. 1:1-2:

> Paul, an apostle of Jesus Christ by the commandment of God our Saviour, and Lord Jesus Christ, which is our hope; Unto Timothy, my own son in the faith: Grace, mercy, and peace, from God our Father and Jesus Christ our Lord.

There is room for you, if you have children or if you do not, to become a spiritual father to those who have none. Timothy had a father, but by all accounts, he was not a follower of Christ. Paul steps in to be the spiritually godly influence in His life. He gives credit to Timothy's mother and grandmother, who were influential in instilling the ways of the Lord early in

Timothy's life. However, Paul understood the necessity of having a godly, manly influence in His life.

2. The Instruction of biblical truths

Paul doesn't only teach Timothy the things that become manliness but teaches him the things that become godliness. He teaches him how to be a leader of men by example, as he follows Christ. Paul's desire was not to just equip Timothy for the here and now, but for eternity. This should be every father's desire. Whether the children around you are your own or spiritually adopted, your desire should be to influence them for eternity!

3. The Lessons that Transcend Time

These same things taught are available to us all today. We must read them, study them, and apply them. Then we must exemplify them to our children so that they too can become what God has called them to be for His kingdom.

I believe Spurgeon stated, "God forbid my son should stoop to be a king, when God has called him to be a preacher." I desire the best for my son. I want His physical needs to be met, but even more than this, I want His spiritual needs to be met. God the Father supplies everything we have need of physically but goes to even greater lengths to make certain we are provided for spiritually. When we were lost and undone, He sent His Son to seek us and save us. When we have those moments of dryness, He sends His Spirit to refresh us. When we are in a fiery trial, He comes and walks with us through it, promising that, although we walk through the fire, we will not be burned. When we are in a fierce battle, He sends in reinforcements to help us become overcomers. The point is that there's nothing that God the Father will not do for those who are truly His. The same is often true of earthly fathers; we are willing to do whatever we can for our children's physical needs, but how much more should we equip them for their spiritual needs!

Third, as a minister of the gospel of Jesus Christ

In the lesson I gave to the young men, I told them they needed to understand something specific. These men were not given these positions first and then they started following these higher standards of godly leadership. They were already living it. These men already held this specific standard for no other reason than that of pleasing God and leading their families in that same path.

We are given twenty-six lifestyle standards that are internal and external. These are all found in 1 Timothy 3:1-7; Titus 1:5-9; 1 Peter 5:1-4.

I. The Calling of Leadership: A Noble and Sacred Task

Paul and Peter affirm that aspiring to spiritual leadership is honorable and God-ordained. It's not a pursuit of status, but a response to divine invitation. Leaders are stewards of God's household, entrusted with care, oversight, and spiritual formation.

When I consider the two words 'noble and sacred' I immediately consider two other words 'honor and weightiness'. I believe that when anyone has been saturated with the burden of being called 'minister' there should within that individual be a sense of humility. A vessel being chosen to not only be poured into, but used to be poured out. However, what should follow this is the understanding that this calling comes with it a greater responsibility than other vocation.

In my book, Confidence in the Call, I write about this great responsibility. We have been called to be watchmen. What we do with this calling, what we know about God from His Word, and how we preach and live this before humanity will be brought before the Judge of all.

The call of God is not for the weak or spineless, nor is it for the proud and arrogant.

May you who feel this urgency swelling inside you answer the call and submit to the authority of Christ' commissioning.

II. Character Over Charisma: The Moral Backbone of a Leader

Across all three texts, the emphasis is unmistakable: integrity is non-negotiable. A leader must be:

- Above reproach—blameless in conduct and reputation
- Faithful in marriage—"husband of one wife," reflecting covenant fidelity
- Temperate, self-controlled, and disciplined—not impulsive or indulgent
- Not arrogant or quick-tempered—humility and patience are essential
- Not a drunkard or violent—gentleness must mark their interactions
- Not greedy or a lover of money—free from materialism and manipulation
- Respectable and hospitable—welcoming and dignified in demeanor
- A lover of good, upright, and holy—morally grounded and spiritually mature

Under this point, we see a very important word, "integrity." As stated it is non-negotiable. Integrity keeps the minister grounded. When people fade round you and you're left alone, when the criticism comes for your stand for truth, and when no one is watching, integrity keeps you. Integrity reminds you whom you're doing this for. Not the crowd. Not the platform. But Christ. It restores your vision when compromise clouds it, and holds you accountable when applause tempts forgetfulness. Integrity is the echo of the Cross in the soul of a leader—it is what keeps your eyes set on Him, your hands clean, and your heart burning."

III. Household as a Mirror: Leadership Begins at Home

Home is the proving ground of spiritual leadership. A leader must:

- Manage their household well—with order, love, and spiritual guidance
- Have believing, submissive children—not rebellious or wild
- Demonstrate maturity—not a recent convert, lest pride take root
- Be well thought of by outsiders—a public witness that honors Christ

I remember the very first time I heard this biblical truth. I was in Royal Rangers, and the devotion was on this very topic.

In the story, a man was being considered to be a deacon in the church, the elders doing the considering acknowledged that the man held all of the qualifications with the exception of one, he had no control of his home. His children were rebellious, and his wife did not respect her husbands position in the hierarchy laid out by God.

The truth made a lasting impression on my heart and mind. From that moment on I understood that my family would impact my calling and so I began to make it a matter of prayer.

Thankfully, the Lord answered the prayers.

Young ministers, please take it from me, I have seen ministries greatly hindered and altogether undone because of their households. Be careful and prayerful about your future.

IV. Doctrinal Soundness: Anchored in the Word

Titus and Timothy stress that leaders must:

- Hold firmly to the trustworthy Word
- Be able to teach sound doctrine
- Refute false teaching with clarity and conviction

V. Shepherding with Humility: The Posture of a True Elder

Peter adds a tender layer: leadership must be exercised not under compulsion, but willingly; not for shameful gain, but eagerly; not domineering, but as examples to the flock. The elder is not a ruler, but a shepherd—modeling Christ's care and humility.

And when the Chief Shepherd appears, faithful leaders will receive an unfading crown of glory.

I understand that not everyone who reads this is a father, and you may not have your father present in your life. Your earthly father may not have had a godly influence. Can I tell you that you have a Heavenly Father to whom you can always call and always count on? You may not have had good influences of godly biblical leadership within the church, but the Word of God stands true and provides a solid blueprint for godliness in leadership.

Men, if I can encourage us to take seriously, to a new height, the great responsibility that we hold. Not only for our own children, but for those children with whom we have an open door of influence. If you know a young person or child in need of a godly influence, you can be the one. And, not only for our children and the children of whom we are to influence to live godly lives but to the entire body of Christ. Anyone who has ears to hear!

You and I are leaving a legacy. I want to leave one that leads to a heavenly eternity.

Fourth, a responsibility to unity

As Christian leaders in the church and community, our responsibility to each other and in the community is directly related to what Christ told His followers. He stated, and I paraphrase, "People will know that you belong to me by your love for one another." You have already read this verse in the previous chapter and will see this verse again, because it is so important in our effectiveness among the Body of Christ and in our communities.

Unity is a thought that has its roots in the Old Testament and is seen even in the creation account.

The psalmist, King David, wrote in Psalm 133:1, "A Song of degrees of David. Behold, how good and how pleasant it is for brethren to dwell together in unity!"

"I have never yet known the Spirit of God to work where the Lord's people were divided" - D.L. Moody.

"Be united with other Christians. A wall with loose bricks is not good. The bricks must be cemented together" - Corrie Ten Boom.

Unity is needed in the church today. When the church is divided, the enemy finds an easy way to infiltrate and destroy it. Disunity is the great hindrance of the miraculous and not only will this destroy the church, but it will also hinder or altogether destroy our witness for Christ among those of whom we have been given the responsibility to reach. We must be unified according to God's Word

I want to look at the Bible and see what God has to tell us about unity.

I. Our Unity is founded in the Trinity...The Father, The Son, and The Holy Ghost.

> Endeavoring to keep the unity of the Spirit in the bond of peace. There is one body, and one **Spirit**, even as ye are called in one hope of your calling; One **Lord**, one faith, one baptism, One **God** and Father of all, who is above all, and through all, and in you all (Eph 4:3-6).

Even as the Father, Son, and Holy Ghost are completely in unity in every way, so should the church, you and I, be! These Three do not disagree and are not divided. They have the same common goal and purpose! Though their offices of duty may differ, the end desire is the same.

> The seat of Christian unity is in the heart or spirit: it does not lie in one set of thoughts, nor in one form and mode of worship, but in one heart and one soul. This unity of heart

and affection may be said to be of the Spirit of God; it is wrought by him, and is one of the fruits of the Spirit. This we should endeavor to keep (Matthew Henry).

II. Our Unity Is Meant For Each Other's Betterment

"Fulfil ye my joy, that ye be likeminded, having the same love, being of one accord, of one mind. Let nothing be done through strife or vainglory (Never be opposed to each other; never act from separate interests; ye are all brethren, and of one body; therefore let every member feel and labor for the welfare of the whole.); but in lowliness of mind (Have always an humbling view of yourselves, and this will lead you to prefer others to yourselves) let each esteem other better than themselves (We must esteem the good which is in others above that which is in ourselves). Look not every man on his own things, but every man also on the things of others. (Do nothing through self-interest in the things of God; nor arrogate to yourselves gifts, graces, and fruits, which belong to others; ye are all called to promote God's glory and the salvation of men.)" (Phip 2:2-4).

Unity key is found in the scripture that we all know as "The Golden Rule. "Therefore all things whatsoever ye would that men should do to you, do ye even so to them: for this is the law and the prophets." (Matthew 7:12).

And also in this: "Finally, be ye all of one mind, having compassion one of another, love as brethren, be pitiful, be courteous:" (1Pe 3:8).

I have never seen a church where unity was present, where the Holy Ghost didn't have liberty. I have never seen a church where unity was present and where spiritual maturity and growth were absent. We need each other, and we need to be in unity, because when we are, we can be more effective for God's kingdom.

III. Our Unity Is Meant To Be a Testimony Of The One We Serve and From Whom We Learn

"By this shall all men know that ye are my disciples, if ye have love one to another." (John 13:35).

When we are in unity and we have love for one another, people will notice.

In a world today where there is disunity and an attitude that says, "It's all about me, myself, and I." It won't take long for people to realize to whom you belong.

Tertullian, in his Apologetic writing, gives us their (sinners looking at the Christian love and unity for one another and others) very words: "See, said they, how they love one another, and are ready to lay down their lives for each other."

"Let this mind be in you, which was also in Christ Jesus:" (Phip 2:5).

We should have the mind of Christ. When we are united with Him, and when we are in unity with one another, people will see and desire that same unity and love exhibited.

IV. Our Unity Is Meant to Last Continually

"Let brotherly love continue." (Hebrews 13:1).

Let it continue in the Good Times! Let it continue in the Bad Times! Let it continue in every Christian and every church! Be all of one heart and one soul. Feel for, comfort, and support each other; and remember that they who profess to love God should love their brother also.

Brothers and Sisters, let us remember what the Lord is telling us! Let us be in unity and love one another. The only way the enemy can win is when we are divided! And when we are divided, it makes it hard for God's Spirit to move.

What does the Bible say about fixing disunity?

Jesus tells us in Mat 5:23-24:

> Therefore if thou bring thy gift to the altar, and there rememberest that thy brother hath ought against thee; Leave there thy gift before the altar, and go thy way; first be reconciled to thy brother, and then come and offer thy gift.

Take care of the problem by forgiving and being forgiven. Move past the division and strive to draw closer to the Lord.

If we expect God to move in our lives, our churches, and our communities, then we must be in unity. If we want to overcome the enemy, then we must be in unity! We must be in unity with one another and more so with the Lord!

Lastly, I AM A WATCHMAN. This, which God had showed me struck me to the core, especially with the great seriousness and gravity of this particular responsibility.

I remember when Christ showed me my responsibility as a spiritual watchman and the great consequences if I didn't fulfill it.

Let's look at the Song of Solomon

> 3:1 By night on my bed I sought him whom my soul loveth: I sought him, but I found him not. 2 I will rise now, and go about the city in the streets, and in the broad ways I will seek him whom my soul loveth: I sought him, but I

> found him not. 3 The watchmen that go about the city found me: to whom I said, Saw ye him whom my soul loveth? 7 The watchmen that went about the city found me, they smote me, they wounded me; the keepers of the walls took away my veil from me.

Matthew Henry Commentary states, "In the night the watchmen go about the city, for the preservation of its peace and safety, to guide and assist the honest and quiet."

These watchmen are similar to what modern-day police or guards are. Yet scripture gives us another way to look at watchmen.

Watchmen, according to scripture, are considered ministers. They watch over the souls of men, calling out danger and issuing good news.

This is the biblical watchman; this is our calling and responsibility.

In our verses mentioned from Song of Solomon, we have three characters.

1. The Seeker – These are those who are looking for truth. They long for the Beloved. They desire to have a relationship with the Beloved. They search, seeking assistance from others to guide them to the One their heart longs for.

2. The Watchmen – These are those who are to assist. They are to have knowledge of the Beloved, they are to possess the truth themselves, and guide the seeker to where they may find it.

3. The Beloved – This is representative of Christ. He is our Beloved. He is Truth. He is the one that every heart longs for, yet is unaware of how or where to find Him.

Our text reveals something very sad and disgraceful, something we should guard against:

The very ones who were to assist ended up being the ones to cause harm and hinder the seeker from finding the beloved.

If we are not careful, by our words, actions, and attitudes, we can hinder and even abuse someone who is seeking truth. We can cause her to stop seeking, we can cause her to even garner a hatred for the Beloved.

Thankfully, the seeker never stopped looking and eventually found her Beloved.

Let us examine Acts 10:

We will see a seeker, a watchman, and the beloved in this story.

> 1 There was a certain man in Caesarea called Cornelius, a centurion of the band called the Italian band, 2 A devout man, and one that

> feared God with all his house, which gave much alms to the people, and prayed to God always. 3 He saw in a vision evidently about the ninth hour of the day an angel of God coming in to him, and saying unto him, Cornelius. 4 And when he looked on him, he was afraid, and said, What is it, Lord? And he said unto him, Thy prayers and thine alms are come up for a memorial before God. 5 And now send men to Joppa, and call for one Simon, whose surname is Peter: 6 He lodgeth with one Simon a tanner, whose house is by the sea side: he shall tell thee what thou oughtest to do. 7 And when the angel which spake unto Cornelius was departed, he called two of his household servants, and a devout soldier of them that waited on him continually; 8 And when he had declared all these things unto them, he sent them to Joppa.

We see Cornelius, a seeker. He had some knowledge, but there was more he needed to know. He needed to know that there was indeed a Savior, the Messiah, who came to die for him and the world.

> 9 On the morrow, as they went on their journey, and drew nigh unto the city, Peter went up upon the housetop to pray about the sixth hour: 10 And he became very hungry,

and would have eaten: but while they made ready, he fell into a trance, 11 And saw heaven opened, and a certain vessel descending unto him, as it had been a great sheet knit at the four corners, and let down to the earth: 12 Wherein were all manner of fourfooted beasts of the earth, and wild beasts, and creeping things, and fowls of the air. 13 And there came a voice to him, Rise, Peter; kill, and eat. 14 But Peter said, Not so, Lord; for I have never eaten any thing that is common or unclean. 15 And the voice spake unto him again the second time, What God hath cleansed, that call not thou common. 16 This was done thrice: and the vessel was received up again into heaven. 17 Now while Peter doubted in himself what this vision which he had seen should mean, behold, the men which were sent from Cornelius had made enquiry for Simon's house, and stood before the gate, 18 And called, and asked whether Simon, which was surnamed Peter, were lodged there. 19 While Peter thought on the vision, the Spirit said unto him, Behold, three men seek thee. 20Arise therefore, and get thee down, and go with them, doubting nothing: for I have sent them.

25 And as Peter was coming in, Cornelius met him, and fell down at his feet, and worshipped him. 26But Peter took him up, saying, Stand up; I myself also am a man. 27And as he talked with him, he went in, and found many that were come together.

> 34 Then Peter opened his mouth, and said, of a truth I perceive that God is no respecter of persons: 35But in every nation he that feareth him, and worketh righteousness, is accepted with him. 36 The word which God sent unto the children of Israel, preaching peace by Jesus Christ: (he is Lord of all:) 37 That word, I say, ye know, which was published throughout all Judaea, and began from Galilee, after the baptism which John preached; 38 How God anointed Jesus of Nazareth with the Holy Ghost and with power: who went about doing good, and healing all that were oppressed of the devil; for God was with him. 39 And we are witnesses of all things which he did both in the land of the Jews, and in Jerusalem; whom they slew and hanged on a tree: 40 Him God raised up the third day, and shewed him openly 41 Not to all the people, but unto witnesses chosen before of God, even to us, who did eat and drink with him after he rose from the dead. 42 And he commanded us to preach unto the people, and to testify that it is

> he which was ordained of God to be the Judge of quick and dead. 43 To him give all the prophets witness, that through his name whosoever believeth in him shall receive remission of sins.

We now have Peter, the watchman. He was called by God to proclaim the truth. He was to assist Cornelius in presenting Christ to him. The Beloved wanted him to know that He was what he needed.

God had to address some things with Peter first. He had to address his prejudice. His assumption that this blessing was only for the Jews had to be dealt with. Now Peter could've responded in a way that could've hindered Cornelius. He could've responded in a way that belittled Cornelius, but after God addressed Peter, Peter was able to say, "God is no respecter of persons." Meaning, God wills to save any and all who will believe, even if they are different from us!

> 44 While Peter yet spake these words, the Holy Ghost fell on all them which heard the word. 45 And they of the circumcision which believed were astonished, as many as came with Peter, because that on the Gentiles also was poured out the gift of the Holy Ghost. 46 For they heard them speak with tongues, and magnify God. Then answered Peter, 47 Can any man forbid water, that these should not be

> baptized, which have received the Holy Ghost as well as we? 48 And he commanded them to be baptized in the name of the Lord. Then prayed they him to tarry certain days.

Because Peter obeyed the voice of God, Cornelius and those with him heard the gospel, were saved, and were filled with the Holy Ghost.

We must get a biblical watchmen mentality. We must be ones who look beyond where someone is and bring them to the Savior! We must be presenters of the Gospel, directing all to Jesus Christ, the beloved! We must not allow our actions, words, or attitudes to cause a hindrance to those who are seeking truth.

If you have read this far, you can see the importance of biblical leadership. Biblically minded leaders are Christ-minded. Biblically minded leaders are governed by the Spirit of God and thus, lead in a biblical way.

Whether you are a future leader or current, whether you are a man or a woman, whether young or old, whether you are a pastor or a lay member. The principles of biblical leadership apply.

CHAPTER

5

BIBLICAL DISCIPLINE

"When discipline leaves the church,
Christ leaves with it"

–Jonathan Hayashi.

"For the commandment is a lamp;
and the law is light; and reproofs of instruction
are the way of life"

(Pro 6:23).

I was scrolling through Facebook, and a post caught my eye. The picture was of an open letter, and the heading of the post read something like, "This is not God!" Upon reading that, I was immediately intrigued, and so naturally I did what any person would do, and I read the letter; then, I moved on to the comments. I've only ever had this happen a handful of times or so, but I instantly became filled with righteous indignation!

What was within the letter, I can't honestly remember. It has been a couple of years since I had read it, but I can remember the gist of what was going on.

The letter was from the elders and the pastor of a church addressed to a lady, who I assume, had been a registered voting member. She had apparently started missing church and started living in sin. Within the letter were the words, "We have tried to schedule a time to meet with you to address our concerns, but you have neglected to respond to our efforts. With your continual rejection of our efforts to talk with you and your living in sin according to (enter scripture reference) we will have no choice but to revoke your membership until repentance and confession have been done."

I read the opinions of "Christians." What followed was a bashing of the church, the elders, the pastor, and a protestation that Christ is only about love.

Now, I will not expound much on my opinion concerning this post that I read, except for this: my righteous indignation wasn't at the church, the pastor, or the elders.

I am persuaded it is of the utmost importance and believe that it is urgent enough to expound on what exactly Biblical Discipline is.

We must first understand and define what discipline is.

Discipline, according to *Merriam-Webster's Dictionary* is to "train someone to obey rules or a code of behavior, using punishment to correct disobedience. It is strict training that corrects or strengthens moral character."

Although this is accurate, we are striving to have the Bible be our foundation and to live in accordance with it. So, we will look at the biblical definition as well.

Discipline is correction aimed at the avoidance of moral fault and the acquisition of moral insight. It is the effort to create moral integrity. The learning of a specific way of life…The way of Christ.

There are three types of discipline:

1. Preventive Discipline – Measure to preempt (curve, cut off) misbehavior.
2. Supportive Discipline – The Training of Self-Control. Teaching the disciplines necessary to avoid the last type of discipline.
3. Corrective Discipline – Consequence(s) for breaking of the rules, guidelines, commands.

These hold a domino effect. If we fail to adhere to God's Preventive Discipline and fail to practice Christ's Supportive Discipline, we will certainly receive the Corrective Discipline.

The Bible does hold all three of the above. You don't have to go very far before you find them, as we will soon discover.

There are "Preventive Disciplines" where God gives written and verbal directives, and with the directive, gives the natural or resulting consequences. There are "Supportive Disciplines" where God tells us how we can practice certain habits that result in the transformation of our hearts, minds, and spirits and bring us into alignment with Him and His word. There are "Corrective Disciplines," examples of how God issued out disciplines, just consequences, when rules were broken.

Let us examine these disciplines biblically:

The first of these is in the very beginning of child rearing. The parent teaches the child, "You can do this, but you cannot do that. If you do that, this is what will happen." I have had such conversations with my own children, and we can see it given by God Himself.

1. Instruction Given

"And the LORD God commanded the man, saying, of every tree of the garden thou mayest freely eat:" (Gen 2:16).

"But of the tree of the knowledge of good and evil, thou shalt not eat of it" (Gen 2:17).

2. Consequence Given

> Continued from verse 17, …"for in the day that thou eatest thereof thou shalt surely die."

The death that is referred to is twofold in nature.

Firstly, it is immediate. It is the result of disobedience to God's commands. It is spiritual death and unless its effects are altered by an outside force (The life-giving blood of Christ alone), it will result in what the Bible calls "the second death"—eternal separation from God. Secondly, it is the natural progression of dilapidation caused by sin, which is known by God alone. Life and death are in the hands of the Lord; it is appointed unto man, once to die. This is the physical death.

God does speak plainly. He lays out what our rebellious first parents need to do, so that ignorance is not an excuse, and equally lays out, in mercy, the consequences of their disobedience so that there are no surprises.

This is Preventative Discipline. God gave instructions for their benefit, so they would not die. "Take fast hold of instruction; let her not go: keep her; for she is thy life" (Pro 4:13).

Another example of Preventive Discipline is that of the Ten Commandments. However, those commands not only gave the consequences for not following them, but also the reward.

Side not for those who might say that "That's O.T. law, which doesn't apply because Christ did away with it." I would draw our attention to Christ's summarizing of the Ten Commandments.

> (Mat 22:36) Master, which is the great commandment in the law?
>
> (Mat 22:37) Jesus said unto him, thou shalt love the Lord thy God with all thy heart, and with all thy soul, and with all thy mind.
>
> (Mat 22:38) This is the first and great commandment.
>
> (Mat 22:39) And the second is like unto it, thou shalt love thy neighbour as thyself.
>
> (Mat 22:40) On these two commandments hang all the law and the prophets.

A Pharisee asks Christ, "Which is the great commandment?" Christ's response was not just a pinpointing of the Great Commandment, but a summarizing of all the commandments. Verse 37 summarizes the first four of the Ten Commandments. The emphasis is on God being our head and our need for commitment to Him. Verse 39 is the summarization of the last six commandments, with the emphasis on our relationship and example to those around us. The last six are possible only by complete obedience to the first four.

The importance of our understanding this is that Christ incorporated what the people knew and understood of the Old Testament to teach them the deeper mysteries of God. Which would open their eyes to the doctrines He would be teaching them.

The second, Sportive Disciplines, are all throughout the scripture. They are for those who have already come to know the Lord and have yielded themselves to Him. My personal emphasis for this section will come from the New Testament.

"Now we have received, not the spirit of the world, but the spirit which is of God; that we might know the things that are freely given to us of God" (1Co 2:12).

"Which things also we speak, not in the words which man's wisdom teacheth, but which the Holy Ghost teacheth; comparing spiritual things with spiritual" (1Co 2:13).

The Wisdom texts tell us that, "The fear of the LORD is the beginning of knowledge" (Proverbs 1:7). What is the fear of the LORD? Reverence. A proper perspective that without Him we are nothing and can know nothing.

This foundation is of the utmost importance in the life of any believer. When we recognize our state, we keep a proper perspective of God, and, when we keep a proper perspective of God, we start the processes of gaining godly wisdom.

The text in 1 Corinthians shows us that is by the Spirit of God alone that we can, "Know the things that are freely given to us of God."

These are not taught by man's wisdom, but by the Holy Ghost alone!

We need to know, also, that to understand these spiritual things, we must be spiritual. One with a carnal mind cannot understand, unless the Holy Ghost calls him to repentance and opens his understanding.

These Supportive Disciplines guide us into truth and instruct us in what is right. These Supportive Disciplines are often lessons that contradict our flesh, but if practiced properly and consistently, they will strengthen the spirit.

There are two types of Supportive Disciplines. I am referencing these two points from The Spirit of the Disciplines by Dallas Willard.

1. Disciplines of Abstinence – These are often less known and harder to practice.
2. Disciplines of Engagement – These are often well known, yet rarely practiced or not fully understood in their importance.

In the first section, there are seven disciplines:

First, Solitude. We are creatures of fellowship. We naturally desire to be around people. People who think like us, feel like us, and believe like us. However, we must take a lesson from our Savior. He often separated Himself to become spiritually fed by the Father. So, if you thought I was referring to being a hermit, you are mistaken. Solitude for the believer is meant to garner spiritual strength. To separate from the world and to become fully committed to Christ. However, we must not forsake "the assembling" together with the saints.

Second, Silence. Now, this is one that is hard. Some people are natural-born talkers. Some are quieter and backwards. Some say they cannot function without having something going on. Silence is the act of shutting out the distractions of the world, such as, shutting off the cell phones and turning off the TV (or YouTube). It is getting to a place where you can hear the still small voice of God, instead of constantly looking for, or rather, being distracted by the neon lights, lightings, thundering, and earthquakes.

Third, Fasting. Now, I am going to say this, and I don't intend to offend anyone. However, this must be said. "Fasting" your favorite drink, gaming console, or social media apps is not biblical fasting. Biblical fasting costs. Biblical fasting involves the giving up of something that is necessary for life. Food and water, exhibited by our Lord, is fasting. Also, fasting shouldn't be done just for any old reason, but for the purpose of the flesh (that nature which often rises up to war against the spiritual man) to die, for the spirit to thrive, and to fashioned into something useful for God. A vessel, meet for the master's use. Fasting is hard, yet I can say from personal experience, I have never felt closer to God than when my flesh is dying. This shows our utter complete reliance on God. My, what would happen if we did more of this?

Fourth, Frugality. This lesson is one that I am still having to learn. Living within your means, instead of keeping up with the Joneses. In a world that is constantly pushing for us to have more, Christ tells us to be content. Work hard, give to the Lord what is His, take care of your family and other responsibilities, and be like the ant and plan for the future. The borrower, who is what many people are, is servant to the lender.

Fifth, Chastity. My pastor, in preaching one service, began to talk about how the world pushes sensuality. It is on every billboard, on every TV commercial, on every radio commercial, on every social media ad. We live in a culture where what God had ordained as a blessing, marriage, has been placed in the gutter and made to be something dirty. Literally, at our fingertips, a crude practice of this sacred action can be viewed, a practice that the world and even those in the church flock after. No commitment. The marriage bed has become defiled. If you are single, practice chastity. Wait for God's perfect one. Don't, for lack of better terminology, date and be sexually active like you try on shoes. Consecrate yourself, save yourself, honor yourself, and those with whom you go into relationships. If you are married, be faithful and committed to your spouse, don't give in to temptation. Don't break sacred trust. Guard yourself and guard your spouse. Strive to keep pure sexuality.

Sixth, Secrecy. There are some things concerning our walk with the Lord that do not need to be public knowledge. This is where this discipline comes into play. Understand, what should not be hidden is the fact that YOU ARE A CHRISTIAN. However, the world doesn't need to know when we perform some tasks. Have you ever seen the videos, which are meant to poke fun, where someone is on a mission trip and they act so humble, yet is very loud about their actions while in the "mission field"? Or how about those people who feel the need to tell everyone that they gave this or did that for the benefit of the church? This is a habit that should be steered clear of, and secrecy should be practiced.

Seventh, Sacrifice. I will use a phrase I have used before and say it often. "The servant is not greater than his Lord" (John 13:16 KJV). This must be understood. We are not above the call to sacrifice. Christ left Heaven's portals, limited Himself into human flesh, felt hunger, thirst, weariness, loneliness, loss, He felt ridicule, hatred, and betrayal, He felt the sting of death. He sacrificed all for us. When He calls for us to sacrifice, we should, with great rejoicing, give our all as well.

For the sake of your time, not to lessen their importance, the next set of disciplines will just be named. The fact is, we know these; they are not unfamiliar to us. We have heard them taught and preached on many times, from Sunday school up. However, the question is, do we practice them faithfully?

First, Study of God's Word. Second, Worship. Third, Celebration. Fourth, Service. Fifth, Prayer. Sixth, Fellowship. Seventh, Confession. Eighth, Submission.

All these disciplines involve our effort and practice. Know that they will not save us; however, they will keep us. They involve our full surrender to the transforming power of Christ, by the Holy Ghost.

They involve Christ being Lord of our lives.

The Last of the three disciplines is the one we are most familiar with and like the least. However, it is also the one discipline which we often have the most issues with.

Biblical Correction is often misunderstood entirely for two reasons:

1. The church believes that correction is primarily for the sinners. However, I would point out that the majority of corrections laid out in Scripture are directed to the church.
2. The church doesn't have a proper understanding of how God has designed correction. No study of God's design often incurs an imbalance of great proportions.

Tolerance: This is a word that has completely saturated our culture and, frankly, has caused a bad taste in the mouths of many people.

The world has a perspective that hates (to some extent) to view anything as bad and deserving of correction. This mentality has even crept in, unaware, into the church.

In the story I shared at the beginning of the chapter, I became increasingly aware of how far removed the church had become from biblical correction and its importance. As I continued to study the topic out for myself, the more aware I became of how rarely, if ever, I had seen biblical correction practiced.

Corrective Discipline is difficult for anyone. No one likes correction; it goes against our very nature. Equally, no one likes to be the 'bad guy' in issuing a correction. However, it is inescapable. You show up to work late enough times, and the likely result will be your termination of employment. If you murder someone, you will likely spend the rest of your days in prison or receive a more final and fatal punishment.

The fact remains, the church has neglected the practice of biblical discipline. Why? For reasons that, in all truth, hold no water. Leaders don't want to offend anyone. They don't want to judge anyone. They don't want to embarrass anyone. Although these may be legitimate reasons, they are not enough to completely ignore the Word of God.

Don't misunderstand, I am not stating that we need to be abusive. Quite the opposite. We are taught throughout the scriptures that gentleness and mercy should be extended.

My mother had a specific method when disciplining my brother and me. She would first have a discourse (I say this jokingly) of why what we did was wrong according to Scripture.

If we lied, my mother told us what God's word said about lying, its consequences, and dangers. Then she would proceed with utilizing the rod, which was in the shape of a bamboo backscratcher, giving us the proper application of her backswing. Then she would move on to praying with us afterwards. However, she always told us the same set of words, "I love you too much to let you continue doing what is wrong. I will give an account before God for not addressing your wrongdoing."

I have since come to greatly appreciate her method and have used the same with my own children when they come to the age of understanding.

Why? The answer is simply this: I want my children to know what God's truth is and to be biblical (apply its teachings).

The reason for this book, this chapter, and this section is that we must regain biblical living, even in how individual or corporate discipline is conducted within the church. To regain an understanding of God's reason and what the Church's motive must be.

First, let us understand what the Bible says about the correction given by God.

God is aware. This must be known. He is completely 'in the know' concerning our actions, thoughts, and intentions.

We need to know that God sees: "The eyes of the LORD are in every place, beholding the evil and the good" (Pro 15:3).

This is something we like to think of when we are doing good, but we somehow manage to forget when we are not doing right. He sees the good and evil. This should be a comfort to us all and equally a challenge. Why? If we understand and remember this, we will be more apt to keep ourselves from straying and doing evil in the sight of the Lord.

We need to know that God knows the human heart: "I the LORD search the heart, I try the reins, even to give every man according to his ways, and according to the fruit of his doings" (Jer 17:10).

"Every way of a man is right in his own eyes: but the LORD pondereth (weighs) the hearts" (Pro 21:2).

There was a picture of a guy that I had seen on Facebook that was being circulated. The man had an emphatic expression on his face, and his hand stretched as if asking why or trying to make a point. If you've seen it, then you know where I'm going with this. The words in the picture state, "Oh, God knows my heart." The man responds, "That should worry you!"

Now, I do not want any to feel as though I am picking on them; however, the church and those within her have taken that one phrase and completely twisted what God was saying to the Prophet Samuel. God sees the heart and knows the heart. We cannot trust our hearts; what comes from our hearts, unless checked by the Spirit of God, only imagines that which is evil. There is nothing hidden, even in the heart.

Scripture tells us, "But if ye will not do so, behold, ye have sinned against the LORD: and be sure your sin will find you out" (Numbers 32:23 KJV).

The point is this: No sin will ever be left unknown nor unaddressed by God. We may escape discipline in this world, but we won't escape discipline in the world to come.

We need to know that God is righteous. "But after thy hardness and impenitent heart treasurest up unto thyself wrath against the day of wrath and revelation of the righteous judgment of God" (Rom 2:5).

We need to know that God is just. "Because he hath appointed a day, in the which he will judge the world in righteousness by that man whom he hath ordained;

whereof he hath given assurance unto all men, in that he hath raised him from the dead" (Act 17:31).

God the Father's justice and righteousness stem from who He is, from His character. He will always do what is right, including allowing us to exercise the free will to do what we want. He will always do what's right by still extending His hand of love and mercy, even through correction. He is righteous through and through, and yet He is still just.

This means He is always consistent. So, as He is consistent in showing mercy and love, He is equally consistent in giving warning that no sin will enter into the Kingdom. He is just and being just when He does so. He will judge sin with consistency and no partiality.

We need to know by whom God will bring just and righteous judgment. "In the day when God shall judge the secrets of men by Jesus Christ according to my gospel" (Rom 2:16).

Why by Jesus? Because Christ's nature is in complete union with God the Father. Because Christ came to this earth to be the supreme and sinless sacrifice for the salvation of mankind. By Christ's words and example, this is how God will judge the "Living and the dead…"

These scriptures alone, which are just a few of many, stand as sufficient evidence for God to bring judgment righteously.

One aspect of God's correction that must be understood, which I referenced in my personal story of how I was corrected as a child, is that God gives correction in love and mercy.

> And ye have forgotten the exhortation which speaketh unto you as unto children, my son, despise not thou the chastening of the Lord, nor faint when thou art rebuked of him
>
> For whom the Lord loveth he chasteneth, and scourgeth every son whom he receiveth (Heb 12:5-6).

The writer of Hebrews reminds the Church that chastisement should not be hated, but a welcomed sigh of relief. As Christians, we have been adopted by God the Father. His desire for us, as His own, is to be eternally secure; so, when the occasion requires, He will give correction to redirect us back to truth. He gives correction because He cares.

"Now no chastening for the present seemeth to be joyous, but grievous: nevertheless, afterward it yieldeth the peaceable fruit of righteousness unto them which are exercised thereby" (Heb 12:11).

Understand, any correction given by God is not unjust. It is for our betterment. It is not done in hate, but only in love. It is not for a temporary purpose, but for an eternal benefit.

As I stated earlier, correction is never enjoyable, but when we consider why correction came, we can rejoice that God is watching for our souls.

Also, we need to acknowledge that when we believers fail and sin. Correction is God's means of bringing about a vindication of His glory, holiness, and His name.

There is no one person in existence who would not desire to restore honor to his name. God the Father, the King of Glory, is no different. As His children and earthly representatives, we should guard our testimony of Him, even in the receiving of correction.

So, how is the church to deal with correction? Is it supposed to? What does the Bible say about it?

In this part of the chapter, we will look intently into what the Bible teaches the church concerning individual and corporate correction.

God has a process in everything. You can see His design even from the very Beginning.

If you look at the following verses in your Bible, you will find that they are written in red. This tells us that these words were not spoken by a mere man, but by the Son of God, Jesus Christ. He gives us the biblical process for correction in the church. Let us read them:

> (Mat 18:15) Moreover if thy brother shall trespass against thee, go and tell him his fault between thee and him alone: if he shall hear thee, thou hast gained thy brother.
>
> (Mat 18:16) But if he will not hear thee, then take with thee one or two more, that in the mouth of two or three witnesses every word may be established.
>
> (Mat 18:17) And if he shall neglect to hear them, tell it unto the church: but if he neglect to hear the church, let him be unto thee as an heathen man and a publican.

Did you see the process? The steps God has ordained by the mouth of His Son?

1. Go in private: We should give each other the benefit of the doubt. Some of the things that we have made mountains out of were nothing more than a misunderstanding. We should go in private to one another and do our part to make it right. The result of handling such things in God's way is that you just might gain a brother or a sister in the Lord. This gaining

involves not wronging the person who might have wronged us.

2. Bring no more than two and no less that one: Christ tells us that, if our brother refuses to hear our correction, refuses to repent, refuses to make amends, then we are to call on one or two individuals. I should state that these individuals should be people of integrity, honesty, spiritual maturity, and completely unbiased. Why? So that there is accountability between you and the individual that is being corrected.

3. Bring it before the church: If the offender refuses to hear you, or the counsel of godly individuals, then bring him before the church. The body often can bring healing even in correction.

4. Consider the individual being corrected as a heathen: After all efforts have been made, after all counsel has been given, if the offender refuses to hear the church, if he refuses to be repentant, he is to be counted as an individual who is lost and no longer in right standing with God. This is hard for us to think about, much less to put into practice. This is in effect the cutting off from fellowship, in a way that would be reserved for brethren in Christ. I

want to make a note here: This is not a cessation of praying and reaching for that individual. As we shall see shortly, effort on the body's part must still be made, for the sake of the disciplined one's eternity.

I am a father of two. My oldest is eight, and my youngest is two. There is something that I was taught, and it actually was from two experiences:

- A conversation that my wife had with her father: She asked him if he, now that he is older, would do things differently in disciplining his children? His response was, "In some things, I would. I think there were times when I was harsher on you four than was necessary for you being just kids."
- My mother was good at this. She purposely took opportunities in our mental, emotional, physical, and spiritual immaturity to teach us. Most people would've gone straight to the rod, but my mother, in patient understanding, taught us.

The point I am making is this: Don't rush to immediate intense correction for spiritual immaturity, especially if the individual is new in the Lord; instead, gently redirect when giving biblical discipleship.

"A man that is an heretick after the first and second admonition reject" (Tit 3:10).

"Knowing that he that is such is subverted, and sinneth, being condemned of himself" (Tit 3:11).

These verses deal with those who are intent on going their own way. Paul is instructing Titus on what measures MUST be taken against those who intend to go their own way. There is to be an effort made to admonish (to gently reprove, to direct in a biblical manner) this individual of the error of his way. This exemplifies the righteous mercy of God shown through godly individuals who are given authority to instruct the errant in righteousness.

Titus was called to be the overseer, ordained as a watchman, and thus had the God-given responsibility of watching out for the souls of men, a responsibility which comes with great consequences if neglected (Hebrews 13:17).

Paul continues, if the errant rejects the admonition, he is subverted (turned over against). He has been turned over to that which causes the heart to become hard, ears to become dull of hearing, and a conscience seared.

Have you ever met anyone who was so intent on doing their own thing that when you tried to give them warning of the dangers of continuing that they rejected what you had to say? This is one who should be left to their own demise according to scripture.

David Guzik states concerning this text that, "Their self-will makes them self-condemned."

This is exemplified throughout scripture with accounts of people who rejected the warnings, instruction, and correction of God by godly people. The ending result was their own demise. Rest assured, any who "does that which is right in his own eyes" will always meet with doom and destruction.

Reader, it is vitally important to make certain that your will is completely submitted to the will of God. He may intervene and save you from yourself. However, He may leave you to yourself and allow you to further separate yourself from Him.

Paul again gives instructions to the church in Rome:

> Now I beseech you, brethren, mark them which cause divisions and offences contrary to the doctrine which ye have learned; and avoid them" (Rom 16:17).

Paul here gives an urgent call to the church. He tells the church to mark those who cause divisions and offences contrary to the doctrines which were already taught.

This is a grave warning to the church to be watchful for false teachings. The church was to mark these and avoid them. Those of the church were to not entertain their words or actions.

This is important for the church to understand because unity in the church is evidence of the present work of God and the indwelling of His Spirit. Without unity, the church will fail. Those who cause division seek the true Church's destruction. Mark them and avoid them!

Paul, in speaking to the Corinthian church, deals with an issue that has permeated the church today.

"It is reported commonly that there is fornication among you, and such fornication as is not so much as named among the Gentiles, that one should have his father's wife" (1 Corinthians 5:1 KJV).

Paul tells them that what he is hearing from within the church should not be happening. He rebukes the sexual immorality and does His due diligence as an apostle, to direct the people's focus to purity and blamelessness.

He tells them that mourning over such a sin should be the outcome, and yet they are puffed up. They looked upon the sin as a light thing. They put minimal degrees upon their sinfulness (this sin is smaller than that sin), when the reality is ALL sin is abhorred by God, the righteous!

Paul says that if the individual remains headstrong and unrepentant then he should be removed, and, in what the world would call extreme, Paul tells the church that the individuals committing these fornications should be delivered unto Satan for the destruction of his flesh, but that his soul might be saved.

"By putting him outside the church, into the world, which is the devil's 'domain.' The punishment is a removal of spiritual protection and social comfort, not an infliction of evil" (David Guzik).

Now, if I may offer my own rebuke to the church: I will do this in the form of a question. How often do sinners come and go from our churches and are not convicted, but, rather, are very much comfortable in both this world of sin and in the church?

This should cause us to grieve and become anguished. This should cause us to remove the "leaven," as Paul states, out of the lump. To remove the things that have caused the church to become contaminated. To become filled with God and His holiness!

This has personally challenged me. May God help the Church and open her eyes!

The great missionary again instructs the Church of the Galatians:

> Brethren, if a man be overtaken in a fault, ye which are spiritual, restore such an one in the spirit of meekness; considering thyself, lest thou also be tempted (Gal 6:1).

I stated earlier that, just because correction must be made and even actions to rebellion against correction must be taken, does not mean we neglect our call to reach and pray for the errant souls.

I have seen men of God and women of God fall. I have seen those whom I once respected become false teachers. I have seen those who, in a moment of weakness, destroy their ministries.

However, I never once rejoiced in their failings. I grieved. I prayed. I sought God. Every time that I did the above, my mind immediately went to the above verse of scripture.

What we must understand about correction is this: It is not about being better. It is not about judging. It is not about being 'holier than thou.' It is about a tug of war for their souls. It is about trying to convince them of what the word of God says concerning what they are doing. It is about fighting against hell, which is eagerly trying to consume them.

Paul, being moved on by the Holy Ghost, instructs us to "restore such a one in the spirit of meekness." Not with our own intellect or goodness. He states, "ye which are spiritual.' What we don't need in the church are unqualified, unspiritual people issuing out correction.

This, I believe, is a big reason why correction in the church has put such a bad taste in people's mouths.

To "restore" doesn't necessarily mean that the person at fault will be put back into the same position or ministry that he once held. However, what it does mean is a restoration of his standing with God. Some may never have the ministry they once had, but they can have a relationship with God and even a better one than they had before.

Paul then tells us the reason we should handle failure among the family of God this way is so that we are not overcome in temptation as well.

In all the evidence above concerning correction in the church, it is for the primary purpose of making sure we are ready for eternity. It is for those of the church as a whole, once again setting their faces upon Christ!

The verse following in Galatians 6:2 declares to us, "Bear ye one another's burdens, and so fulfil the law of Christ."

This is the responsibility of the church. Encourage biblical living, give warning of error, and do all of this with mercy in mind. By doing this, we fulfill the law of Christ in (John 13:34). "A new commandment I give unto you, that ye love one another; as I have loved you, that ye also love one another" (John 13:35). "By this shall all men know that ye are my disciples, if ye have love one to another."

Now, before we end this chapter, I would like to give some instructions to the recipients of correction, including myself.

First, know that any correction must be prayerfully considered. If you are not willing to examine yourself in the mirror of God's Word, then you will never be able to receive correction. If correction applies and aligns with God's word, then take it with thanksgiving, knowing that it is creating you as a life yielded to Christ.

Second, know that not everyone is out to hurt you by correcting you. You may not like it but take the time to ask yourself these questions. "What is their motive? Have they ever lied to me before? Have I seen inconsistency in their life? Are they living biblically?" Never jump to the conclusion that they are out to get you.

This is yours and my responsibility. The reality is this: If we expect to grow in Christ, we will receive correction and pray what the psalmist prayed in Psalm 139:23, "Search me, O God, and know my heart: try me, and know my thoughts."

In fact, if we let God correct us, we would not need the correction of man.

CHAPTER

6

BIBLICAL DOCTRINE

"If we don't know the bible; if we don't know the doctrine; if we don't know the theology, it is virtually impossible for us to identify false prophets"

- Voddie Baucham.

I remember being in a camp meeting when I was a pre-teen. I remember that the Lord had moved so mightily throughout the week, and we had come to the last service. The same preacher preached the entire week and gave no indication of saying anything amiss. However, the very last service was met with a mixture of spiritual grief and physical sickness. Why? The wolf in sheep's clothing began preaching a false doctrine.

Now, at that point in time, I wasn't fully knowledgeable (I'm still probably not), but I was filled with the Holy Ghost, and I had been taught a great deal of truth. I became aware early on of the necessity of knowing the doctrines of Christ.

Thankfully, the leadership of the camp meeting and the host pastor made it a point to point out the man's heresy and admonish the church to reject what he had said.

"Ye therefore, beloved, seeing ye know these things before, beware lest ye also, being led away with the error of the wicked, fall from your own stedfastness" (2 Pet 3:17).

I had been taught, therefore I knew. I was cautious, so I was not led astray into error with the wicked.

Doctrine is that which has been taught. However, a distinction must be made. This is not man's teaching. Why? Because man is fallible. We are not all-knowing. We are not all seeing. We are not all powerful.

So, biblical doctrine is everything concerning the attributes of God. It is all He has done and spoken. It is all He commanded

God is, and He has given instruction and taught mankind, through the avenue of His Word, the way we are to live to be in right standing with Him.

Scripture tells us often to "beware" of false teachers/prophets, and what it is telling us is to be cautious and alert of the dangers of something or even someone.

"Beware of false prophets, which come to you in sheep's clothing, but inwardly they are ravening wolves" (Mat 7:15).

Christ here gives out a warning of caution. He is descriptive of those who are false prophets…they are "ravening wolves."

These false prophets are those who feign holiness and righteousness, yet they are pretenders. Their purpose is to guide away from the doctrines of Christ, from His pathway.

They are ravening, constantly ferocious. They will attempt to devour their prey and be as empty-bellied as before; this drives them onward to their next victim.

Christ instructs us that these false prophets will disguise themselves, even believing their own lie. So, sober-mindedness is an absolute necessity.

"That the aged men be sober, grave, temperate, sound in faith, in charity, in patience" (Tit 2:2).

To be sober-minded is to have a seriousness and clarity to your spiritual walk and to not only possess but put into practice discernment.

Again, Christ issues out a warning. This is a call to use caution with those who are religious. They are those who are learned in the things of God, and yet they have not allowed the Truth to take ahold of them.

"Then Jesus said unto them, Take heed and beware of the leaven of the Pharisees and of the Sadducees" (Mat 16:6).

The Pharisees and the Sadducees were not satisfied with what God had told them; they had to add man-made philosophies, dress them as necessary to serve God, and enforce mankind to follow these ritualistic practices all the while consistently neglecting the things of far greater spiritual importance. It is as if they were saying, "we are so righteous that what God has declared that we need to do is thoroughly insufficient; so, we must add more to bring up to par what God has already said."

To this point I have stated the necessity of being watchful for false teachers and false doctrines. However, what must equally be understood is that we can cause spiritual damage to our own selves by our lack of studying to understand the Word of God.

There has been a plague of—for lack of better terminology—laziness among "Christians". What I mean by this is there has been a reliance solely on the preacher to tell us what God's Word says (as he should), yet they never crack open the Book to cross reference and verify that what the preacher is saying is the truth.

"Bad doctrines act in the soul as leaven does in meal; they assimilate the whole spirit to their own nature" – Adam Clarke.

It is impossible to add ungodly and unbiblical things to our lives and they not corrupt the godly character within us. To illustrate this, an apple that is beginning to rot in a basket full of apples, unless it is removed and the other apples cleansed, will begin to affect the other apples. We must adhere to biblical doctrines alone.

So, how do we guard against false doctrine? By knowing true doctrine. How do we know true doctrine? We dive, headlong, into the Word of Truth. We study to know who God is and what He expects. Like the old song says, "Look! It's in there! Right in the Word of God!"

I have been asked several times over the years, "What is the best way to study the Bible?" The short answer – PRAY AND READ IT!

A slightly longer answer is "Pray that God would show you His word as He wants you to see it in this period of your life and that there would come a growing love for His Word. Carefully read, and, while reading, write down questions you have about words, practices, places, times, and people. Look at Bible dictionaries and commentaries. (There is a good chance that if most of the commentators agree on certain passages of the Bible, they are right in their agreed interpretation.) Seek counsel from the elders who have made it their life's goal to study and know the Scripture. Lastly, pray again at how you are to apply the Word of God to your life."

Let us examine what the Word of God teaches concerning Biblical Doctrine.

1. Sound doctrine should be preached and recognized as completely sufficient for all seasons of life. While there will be some who seek for that which is self-gratifying, for the believer, sound doctrine should be the compass with which we are guided to that eternal place of rest.

   Preach the word; be instant in season, out of season; reprove, rebuke, exhort with all longsuffering and doctrine. For the time will come when they will not endure sound doctrine; but after their own lusts shall they heap to themselves teachers, having itching ears; And they shall turn away their ears from the truth, and shall be turned unto fables (2 Timothy 4:2-4).

2. Sound doctrine should be held fast, closely, and unwaveringly. Holding fast is coupled with the idea that the believer is to "Study to shew thyself approved unto God, a workman that needeth not to be ashamed, rightly dividing the word of truth" (2 Tim. 2: 15). When we study sound doctrine and hold it fast in our souls, we are prepared for the defense of the Gospel and for the answering of the questions concerning the "reason of the hope that is in you" (Titus 1:9). Holding fast the faithful Word as he hath been taught, Titus would be able by sound doctrine both to exhort and to convince the gainsayers.

3. Sound doctrine is to the believer a "lifesaver" in a world that is drowning. When we listen, I mean really listen, and we live within those doctrines, we save ourselves. Yet, we also have the opportunity to rescue others by our living and preaching sound doctrine. "Take heed unto thyself, and unto the doctrine; continue in them: for in doing this thou shalt both save thyself, and them that hear thee" (1 Timothy 4:16).

4. Sound doctrine ought to be the life of the true believer. He should teach and speak about

doctrines and teachings that align with and promote sound, healthy, and true Christian beliefs. This involves focusing on teachings that reflect the true nature of the Gospel and encourage righteous and godly living among believers. "But speak thou the things which become sound doctrine" (Titus 2:1).

Whether your church is independent or a part of a denomination, if true, it will hold to and be guided by biblical doctrines which it believes are absolutely necessary for the church to fulfill its biblical mandate to unity in the body of Christ and fulfillment of "The Great Commission."

1. The Scriptures Inspired: The Bible is the inspired and infallible Word of God, serving as the ultimate authority for faith and conduct. Divine Origin: "All scripture is given by inspiration of God, and is profitable for doctrine, for reproof, for correction, for instruction in righteousness" (2 Timothy 3:16 KJV). Paul exhorted Timothy, "Continue in these things *because the Bible comes from God and not man.* It is a God-inspired book, breathed out from God Himself."

   i. This means something more than saying that God inspired the men who wrote it, though we believe that He did; God also inspired the very words they wrote. We notice it doesn't say, "All

Scripture writers are inspired by God," even though that was true. Yet, it doesn't go far enough. *The words they wrote were breathed by God.*

ii. It isn't that God breathed *into* the human authors. That is true, but not what Paul says here. He says that God breathed out of them His Holy Word" (David Guzik).

2. Role of the Holy Spirit: "Knowing this first, that no prophecy of the scripture is of any private interpretation. For the prophecy came not in old time by the will of man: but holy men of God spake as they were moved by the Holy Ghost" (2 Peter 1:20-21 KJV).

    Far from inventing the subject of their own predictions, the ancient prophets did not even know the meaning of what they themselves wrote. They were carried beyond themselves by the influence of the Divine Spirit, and after ages were alone to discover the object of the prophecy; and the fulfillment was to be the absolute proof that the prediction was of God and that it was of no private invention (Clarke).

    David Guzik notes that the ancient Greek word translated "moved" has the sense of carried along, as a ship being carried along by the wind or the current (the same word is used of a ship in Act

27:15; Act 27:17). "It is as if the writers of Scripture "raised their sails" in cooperation with God and the Holy Spirit carried them along in the direction He wished."

3. Inerrancy and Infallibility: "The words of the Lord are pure words: as silver tried in a furnace of earth, purified seven times." (Psalm 12:6, KJV). "Every word of God is pure: he is a shield unto them that put their trust in him" (Proverbs 30:5, KJV).

   The doctrine of inerrancy asserts that the Scriptures, in their original manuscripts, are without error or contradiction. Infallibility means that the Bible is completely trustworthy and reliable in all it affirms.

   "The law of the Lord is perfect, converting the soul: the testimony of the Lord is sure, making wise the simple" (Psalm 19:7, KJV).

4. Purpose of Scripture: The inspired Scriptures serve multiple purposes: teaching, correcting, training in righteousness, and equipping believers for every good work.

   "For whatsoever things were written aforetime were written for our learning, that we through patience and comfort of the scriptures might have hope" (Romans 15:4, KJV).

Adam Clarke writes:

> From what he says here of them, we learn that God had not intended them merely for those generations in which they were first delivered, but for the instruction of all the succeeding generations of mankind. That we, through patience and comfort of the scriptures - that we, through those remarkable examples of patience exhibited by the saints and followers of God, whose history is given in those scriptures, and the comfort which they derived from God in their patient endurance of sufferings brought upon them through their faithful attachment to truth and righteousness, might have hope that we shall be upheld and blessed as they were, and our sufferings become the means of our greater advances in faith and holiness, and consequently our hope of eternal glory be the more confirmed.

5. Jesus' View of Scripture: Jesus affirmed the inspiration and authority of the Scriptures. He frequently quoted the Old Testament and taught its fulfillment through His life and ministry.

   Matthew 5:17-18 (KJV) Think not that I am come to destroy the law, or the prophets: I am not come to destroy, but to fulfil. For verily I say unto you, Till heaven and earth pass, one jot or one tittle shall in no wise pass from the law, till all be fulfilled.

The inspiration of Scripture means that the Bible is not merely a human document but a divine revelation, providing guidance, truth, and wisdom for believers.

6. The One True God: There is one true God, eternally existent in three persons: Father, Son, and Holy Spirit.

    1. **The Oneness of God – Deuteronomy 6:4 (KJV)** Hear, O Israel: The Lord our God is one Lord.

    2. **The Father is God – Ephesians 4:6 (KJV)**:

One God and Father of all, who is above all, and through all, and in you all.

    3. **The Son (Jesus Christ) is God – John 1:1, 14 (KJV)**:

In the beginning was the Word, and the Word was with God, and the Word was God... And the Word was made flesh, and dwelt among us, (and we beheld his glory, the glory as of the only begotten of the Father,) full of grace and truth.

Colossians 2:9 (KJV): For in him dwelleth all the fulness of the Godhead bodily.

4. **The Holy Spirit is God – Acts 5:3-4 (KJV)**: But Peter said, Ananias, why hath Satan filled thine heart to lie to the Holy Ghost, and to keep back part of the price of the land? ... thou hast not lied unto men, but unto God.

5. **The Three Persons Together – Matthew 3:16-17 (KJV)**: Jesus' Baptism - And Jesus, when he was baptized, went up straightway out of the water: and, lo, the heavens were opened unto him, and he saw the Spirit of God descending like a dove, and lighting upon him: And lo a voice from heaven, saying, This is my beloved Son, in whom I am well pleased.

   Matthew 28:19 (KJV): The Great Commission - Go ye therefore, and teach all nations, baptizing them in the name of the Father, and of the Son, and of the Holy Ghost:

   2 Corinthians 13:14 (KJV): Paul's Benediction: (2Co 13:14) The grace of the Lord Jesus Christ, and the love of God, and the communion of the Holy Ghost, be with you all. Amen. The second epistle to the Corinthians was written from

Philippi, a city of Macedonia, by Titus and Lucas.

At this juncture, I would like to stop and would like to bolster the trinitarian belief with scripture.

Elohim – H430 in the Strong's concordance – Divine plurality. Found within the very first chapter of Genesis in the creation story. God the Father has a meeting with God the Son and God the Holy Ghost and they three in unison make mankind.

In (Gen 1:26), "And God said, Let us make man in our image, after our likeness: and let them have dominion over the fish of the sea, and over the fowl of the air, and over the cattle, and over all the earth, and over every creeping thing that creepeth upon the earth."

The Preacher's Homiletical states that this, "Consultation was Divine. It was a consultation held by the three persons of the ever Blessed Trinity, who were one in the creative work."

Chuck Smith Commentary states, "The tri-unity of God is found in the first verse of the Bible, "in the beginning God," the word in Hebrew is "Elohim". Elohim is a plural word. Other places in the Old Testament it is translated Gods. "El" is God in Hebrew, singular. In Hebrew there is a dual tense, two, and the Hebrew "Elah" is God in a dual tense.

But "Elohim" is the plural tense for God. And so, even the tri-unity of God is expressed in the first verse, "in the beginning God," Elohim. Not "El", but "Elohim" created the heavens and the earth."

In looking at (John 1:1) "In the beginning was the Word, and the Word was with God, and the Word was God."

(John 1:2) The same was in the beginning with God.

(John 1:3) All things were made by him; and without him was not any thing made that was made.

Reading verses like the above, it becomes increasingly clear that the Word of God supports the Trinity doctrine.

David Guzik writes in his commentary, "And the Word was with God, and the Word was God: With this brilliant statement, John 1:1 sets forth one of the most basic foundations of our faith - the Trinity. We can follow John's logic:

- There is a Being known as the Word.
- This Being is God, because He is eternal (In the beginning).
- This Being is God, because He is plainly called God (the Word was God).

- At the same time, this Being does not encompass all that God is. God the Father is a distinct Person from the Word (the Word was with God).

So, the Father and the Son (the Son is known here as the Word) are equally God, yet distinct in their Person. The Father is not the Son, and the Son is not the Father. Yet they are equally God, with God the Holy Spirit making one God in three Persons."

Dr. David Lamb, in his book, Absolute Trinity (A Refutation of the Jesus Only Movement) writes, "The Trinity is to never be viewed as three separate gods, which doctrine is called tri-theism." He states that the reason it is spouted that this is the belief of Trinitarians is for two reasons of which I agree!

First, Trinitarians have done a poor job defending their faith. Second, the deceitfulness of the Oneness preachers' hearts and their willingness to say anything necessary to proselytize.

It would behoove us to 'rightly divide the word of truth' so that we are not bring a shame upon the Gospel of Jesus.

Dr. David Lamb continue, "The Father, Son, and the Holy Ghost share the identical divined substance (John 10:30, Hebrews 1:3, 1 John 5:7), indwell one another (John 10:38, 17:20-22), and occupy the same divine space at the same exact time (Proverbs 15:3, Matthew 18:20, Psalm 139:7).

I would like to encourage you reader to obtain Bro. Lamb's book and read it carefully, checking it with the scriptures, and being armed to defend your faith.

A portion of Scripture, although some would say that this is not in the original, is found in (1Jn 5:7) For there are three that bear record in heaven, the Father, the Word, and the Holy Ghost: and these three are one.

David Guzik writes notes that while it may not be in any original manuscripts, "…it is woven into the fabric of the New Testament - we find the Father, Son, and Holy Spirit working together as equal, yet distinct Persons (Mat 3:16-17; Mat 28:19; Luk 1:35; John 1:33-34; John 14:16, John 14:26; John 16:13-15; John 20:21-22; Acts 2:33-38; Rom 15:16; 2Cor 1:21-22; 2Cor 13:14; Gal 4:6; Eph 3:14-16; Eph 4:4-6; 1Pet 1:2)."

Lastly, I always go to the words written in red. These are words which we all would agree should be able to stand alone. Our Savior, in giving final instructions to the disciples spoke these words to them (Mat 28:19): "Go ye therefore, and teach all nations, baptizing them in the name of the Father, and of the Son, and of the Holy Ghost."

"The experience of God in these three Persons is the essential basis of discipleship. At the same time the singular noun name (not 'names') underlines the unity of the three Persons" (France)

John Gill wrote, "By the authority of these three divine persons, who all appeared, and testified their approbation of the administration of this ordinance, at the baptism of Christ: and as they are to be invocated in it, so the persons baptized not only profess faith in each divine person, but are devoted to their service, and worship, and are laid under obligation to obedience to them, Hence a confirmation of the doctrine of the Trinity, there are three persons, but one name, but one God, into which believers are baptized; and a proof of the true deity both of the Son, and of the Holy Ghost; and that Christ, as the Son of God, is God; since baptism is administered equally in the name of all three, as a religious ordinance, a part of divine instituted worship, which would never be in the name of a creature."

7. The Deity of the Lord Jesus Christ: Jesus Christ is the eternal Son of God, fully divine and fully human.

    1. Jesus' Divine Titles – John 1:1, 14 (KJV): In the beginning was the Word, and the Word was with God, and the Word was God... And the Word was made flesh, and dwelt among

us, (and we beheld his glory, the glory as of the only begotten of the Father,) full of grace and truth.

2. Jesus' Equality with God – John 10:30 (KJV): I and my Father are one.

3. Jesus' Preexistence – John 8:58 (KJV): Jesus said unto them, Verily, verily, I say unto you, Before Abraham was, I am.

4. Jesus' Authority to Forgive Sins – Mark 2:5-7 (KJV): When Jesus saw their faith, he said unto the sick of the palsy, Son, thy sins be forgiven thee. But there was certain of the scribes sitting there, and reasoning in their hearts, Why doth this man thus speak blasphemies? Who can forgive sins but God only?

5. Jesus' Acceptance of Worship – Matthew 14:33 (KJV): Then they that were in the ship came and worshipped him, saying, of a truth thou art the Son of God.

6. Jesus' Divine Works – Colossians 1:16-17 (KJV): For by him were all things created, that are in heaven, and that are in earth, visible and invisible, whether they be thrones, or dominions, or principalities, or powers: all things were created by him, and for him: And

he is before all things, and by him all things consist.

7. Jesus' Identification as God through man– Thomas' Declaration: John 20:28 (KJV): And Thomas answered and said unto him, My Lord and my God.

Peter's Declaration – Mat 16:16 (KJV) And Simon Peter answered and said, Thou art the Christ, the Son of the living God.

8. The Fall of Man: Humanity was created good but fell from grace through disobedience, resulting in physical and spiritual death.

   Romans 3:23: "For all have sinned, and come short of the glory of God."

   Romans 5:12: "Wherefore, as by one man sin entered into the world, and death by sin; and so death passed upon all men, for that all have sinned."

   Ephesians 2:3: "Among whom also we all had our conversation in times past in the lusts of our flesh, fulfilling the desires of the flesh and of the mind; and were by nature the children of wrath, even as others."

   This is often one of the areas that mankind has a problem with being willing to admit. That mankind is inherently wicked. Yet, it is the recognition of this reality which opens up the door for redemption to happen.

9. The Salvation of Man: Salvation is available through Jesus Christ's sacrificial death and resurrection, and it involves repentance, faith, and regeneration by the Holy Spirit.

   John 3:16 (KJV): "For God so loved the world, that he gave his only begotten Son, that whosoever believeth in him should not perish, but have everlasting life."

   Ephesians 2:8-9 (KJV): "For by grace are ye saved through faith; and that not of yourselves: it is the gift of God: Not of works, lest any man should boast."

   Romans 10:9 (KJV): "That if thou shalt confess with thy mouth the Lord Jesus, and shalt believe in thine heart that God hath raised him from the dead, thou shalt be saved."

   Not by our own merits or efforts but wholly by the sacrifice of Jesus Christ on the cross. His blood spilt for you and I.

   I often look at this pivotal moment in time as the time when death gave way to life, darkness bowed before the light, and hopelessness retreated as

Hope rose to stand as a lighthouse to all who would come.

10. The Ordinances of the Church: Water baptism by immersion and Holy Communion are instituted by Christ as symbols of faith and practice.

    Matthew 28:19: "Go ye therefore, and teach all nations, baptizing them in the name of the Father, and of the Son, and of the Holy Ghost."

    Matthew 26:26-28: "And as they were eating, Jesus took bread, and blessed it, and brake it, and gave it to the disciples, and said, Take, eat; this is my body. And he took the cup, and gave thanks, and gave it to them, saying, Drink ye all of it; For this is my blood of the new testament, which is shed for many for the remission of sins."

    1 Corinthians 11:23-26: "For I have received of the Lord that which also I delivered unto you, That the Lord Jesus the same night in which he was betrayed took bread: And when he had given thanks, he brake it, and said, Take, eat: this is my body, which is broken for you: this do in remembrance of me. After the same manner also he took the cup, when he had supped, saying, This cup is the new testament in my blood: this do ye, as oft as ye drink it, in remembrance of me. For as often as ye eat this bread, and drink this cup, ye do shew the Lord's death till he come."

At this point I would like to deviate for just a moment and extend to you for your personal pondering. Paul in his instruction to the Corinthians, under the unction of Holy Ghost, gives an admonition to them concerning the partaking of the communion. It calls for self-examination. "However, this is not written with the thought of excluding ourselves from the table, but of preparing us to receive with the right heart" David Guzik

As a pastor, I feel it is my responsibility to bring this to the churches attention with each time the communion is partaken of.

Taking Christ commands as our foundation for the 'why' let us look at this doctrine not in strictly a traditional sense, but in one of the greatest forms of praise and adoration for our redeemer and Lord.

11. The Baptism in the Holy Spirit: Believers should seek the baptism in the Holy Spirit, which empowers them for service and witness.

A great pivotal foundational piece of the Pentecostal church.

It must be fully understood, that while we may be of service in some aspect unto the Lord without the infilling of the Holy Ghost, we will never be fully equipped unless we are inundated by Him. I am not stating that you have to be, but I am stating that for any believer to be exactly what God has called him to be, he must earnestly seek to be that and strive to be filled with the Holy Ghost.

I would encourage you to read three pieces on this topic and the topic that follows. (12 and 13). First, the entirety of the book of Acts. This book of the early church provides the blueprint for the biblical church. Second, read Dr. Timothy Laurito's book Pentecostal Perspectives: A Guide for Faith and Practice. Third, read Dr. Laurito's second book Speaking in Tongues: A Multidisciplinary Defense, as well as his book, Pentecostal Perspectives.

12. The Initial Physical Evidence of the Baptism in the Holy Spirit: Speaking in tongues, as experienced on the Day of Pentecost, is considered the initial evidence of the Baptism in the Holy Spirit.

13. Sanctification: Sanctification is the process of being set apart for God's purposes, involving both a positional and progressive work of grace.

"For this is the will of God, even your sanctification, that ye should abstain from fornication: That every one of you should know how to possess his vessel in sanctification and honour." (1 Thessalonians 4:3-4).

"And the very God of peace sanctify you wholly; and I pray God your whole spirit and soul and body be preserved blameless unto the coming of our Lord Jesus Christ." (1 Thessalonians 5:23).

"By the which will we are sanctified through the offering of the body of Jesus Christ once for all." (Hebrews 10:10).

"For by one offering he hath perfected for ever them that are sanctified." (Hebrews 10:14).

"Sanctify them through thy truth: thy word is truth." (John 17:17).

"And such were some of you: but ye are washed, but ye are sanctified, but ye are justified in the name of the Lord Jesus, and by the Spirit of our God." (1 Corinthians 6:11).

Sanctification in these scriptures emphasizes the process of being made holy, set apart for God's purposes, and the transformative work of the Holy Spirit in the life of a believer.

14. The Church and ts Mission: The Church is the Body of Christ and is called to worship, evangelize, disciple, and demonstrate God's love.

> And Jesus came and spake unto them, saying, All power is given unto me in heaven and in earth. Go ye therefore, and teach all nations, baptizing them in the name of the Father, and of the Son, and of the Holy Ghost: Teaching them to observe all things whatsoever I have commanded you: and, lo, I am with you alway, even unto the end of the world. Amen (Matthew 28:18-20 KJV).

"The Great Commission is not an option to be considered; it is a command to be obeyed" – Hudson Taylor

I think we often get so caught up in the "how" and "where" that we forget that we were simply told to "Go!" Many say, "I'm not called to be a missionary, preacher, or teacher." My response to this will always be, "Perhaps, you are right, but you are called to be a witness. So, make sure you are doing the best you can to declare Jesus to all. To give good evidence of the God you serve."

15. The Ministry: Divinely called and scripturally ordained ministers lead the Church in fulfilling its mission.

CONCERNING DEACONS:

Likewise must the deacons be grave, not doubletongued, not given to much wine, not greedy of filthy lucre;

Holding the mystery of the faith in a pure conscience.

And let these also first be proved; then let them use the office of a deacon, being found blameless.

Even so must their wives be grave, not slanderers, sober, faithful in all things.

Let the deacons be the husbands of one wife, ruling their children and their own houses well.

For they that have used the office of a deacon well purchase to themselves a good degree, and great boldness in the faith which is in Christ Jesus (1 Timothy 3:8-13).

And in those days, when the number of the disciples was multiplied, there arose a murmuring of the Grecians against the Hebrews, because their widows were neglected in the daily ministration. Then the twelve called the multitude of the disciples unto them, and said, It is not reason that we should leave the word of God, and serve tables.

Wherefore, brethren, look ye out among you seven men of honest report, full of the Holy Ghost and wisdom, whom we may appoint over this business.

But we will give ourselves continually to prayer, and to the ministry of the word.

And the saying pleased the whole multitude: and they chose Stephen, a man full of faith and of the Holy Ghost, and Philip, and Prochorus, and Nicanor, and Timon, and Parmenas, and Nicolas a proselyte of Antioch: Whom they set before the apostles: and when they had prayed, they laid their hands on them (Acts 6:1-6).

CONCERNING ELDERS:

Let the elders that rule well be counted worthy of double honour, especially they who labour in the word and doctrine." (1 Timothy 5:17).

For this cause left I thee in Crete, that thou shouldest set in order the things that are wanting, and ordain elders in every city, as I had appointed thee:

If any be blameless, the husband of one wife, having faithful children not accused of riot or unruly.

For a bishop must be blameless, as the steward of God; not selfwilled, not soon angry, not given to wine, no striker, not given to filthy lucre;

But a lover of hospitality, a lover of good men, sober, just, holy, temperate;

Holding fast the faithful word as he hath been taught, that he may be able by sound doctrine both to exhort and to convince the gainsayers (Titus 1:5-9).

The elders which are among you I exhort, who am also an elder, and a witness of the sufferings of Christ, and also a partaker of the glory that shall be revealed:

Feed the flock of God which is among you, taking the oversight thereof, not by constraint, but willingly; not for filthy lucre, but of a ready mind;

Neither as being lords over God's heritage, but being ensamples to the flock (1 Peter 5:1-3).

CONCERNING BISHOPS:

This is a true saying, If a man desire the office of a bishop, he desireth a good work. A bishop then must be blameless, the husband of one wife, vigilant, sober, of good behaviour, given to hospitality, apt to teach; Not given to wine, no striker, not greedy of filthy lucre; but patient, not a brawler, not covetous;

One that ruleth well his own house, having his children in subjection with all gravity; (For if a man know not how to rule his own house, how shall he take care of the church of God?)

Not a novice, lest being lifted up with pride he fall into the condemnation of the devil. Moreover he must have a good report of them which are without; lest he fall into reproach and the snare of the devil (1Timothy 3:1-7).

For a bishop must be blameless, as the steward of God; not selfwilled, not soon angry, not given to wine, no striker, not given to filthy lucre;

But a lover of hospitality, a lover of good men, sober, just, holy, temperate; Holding fast the faithful word as he hath been taught, that he may be able by sound doctrine both to

> exhort and to convince the gainsayers (Titus 1:7-9).

These qualifications emphasize the importance of character, integrity, and spiritual maturity in church leadership, ensuring leaders can effectively guide and nurture their communities. Now, while some may attempt to interpret these, even as I did in the previous chapter, it is important to note how serious God is concerning leaders in the church.

16. Divine Healing: Healing is provided in Christ's atonement and is available to believers.

> But he was wounded for our transgressions, he was bruised for our iniquities: the chastisement of our peace was upon him; and with his stripes we are healed (Isaiah 53:5 KJV).

> Is any sick among you? let him call for the elders of the church; and let them pray over him, anointing him with oil in the name of the Lord: And the prayer of faith shall save the sick, and the Lord shall raise him up; and if he have committed sins, they shall be forgiven him (James 5:14-15 KJV).

The doctrine of divine healing is a belief that God has the power to heal physical, emotional, and spiritual ailments through supernatural intervention.

There are countless stories of individuals who have experienced this healing: some, I have even seen myself. What is important to know is that God has no limitations. M.D.s can assist with most physical issues. Psychologists can help in some mental and emotional issues. Sometimes these doctors can only assist with the symptoms of our problems. God, however, not only knows the why and the how of what is going on, but also has the answer. He is able to do "exceedingly, abundantly above all we could ask or think, according to the power that worketh in us!"

17. The Blessed Hope: The imminent return of Christ to gather His Church, also known as the Rapture, is the hope of believers.

    "Looking for that blessed hope, and the glorious appearing of the great God and our Saviour Jesus Christ" (Titus 2:13 KJV).

18. The Millennial Reign of Christ: Christ will return with His saints to reign on earth for a thousand years, bringing peace and righteousness.

    > And I saw thrones, and they sat upon them, and judgment was given unto them: and I saw the souls of them that were beheaded for the witness of Jesus, and for the word of God, and which had not worshipped the beast, neither his image, neither had received his mark upon their foreheads, or in their hands;

and they lived and reigned with Christ a thousand years (Revelation 20:4 KJV).

19. The Final Judgment: There will be a Final Judgment where the wicked will be condemned to eternal punishment and the righteous will receive eternal reward.

    And I saw a great white throne, and him that sat on it, from whose face the earth and the heaven fled away; and there was found no place for them. And I saw the dead, small and great, stand before God; and the books were opened: and another book was opened, which is the book of life: and the dead were judged out of those things which were written in the books, according to their works (Revelation 20:11-12 KJV).

20. The New Heavens and the New Earth: God will create a New Heaven and a New Earth where righteousness dwells forever.

    And I saw a new heaven and a new earth: for the first heaven and the first earth were passed away; and there was no more sea. And I John saw the holy city, new Jerusalem, coming down from God out of heaven, prepared as a bride adorned for her husband. And I heard a great voice out of heaven saying, Behold, the tabernacle of God is with men, and he will

> dwell with them, and they shall be his people, and God himself shall be with them, and be their God (Revelation 21:1-3 KJV).

These last four doctrines of the Church give a great deal of hope and expectation to the body of Christ.

Songs are written, speaking of this Blessed Hope. In *Amazing Grace,* it says, "When we've been there ten thousand years, bright shining as the sun, we've no less days to sing God's praise than when we first begun."

Poems speak of this celestial home of the redeemed. Stories, words on paper, pour forth the imaginations of our deepest longings.

Truly, this is the eternal aspect of being free from sin, pain, sorrow, and death. The prospect of being with our Redeemer and the saints who have gone before us draws us and stirs a longing within our souls.

The significance of our Blessed Hope is that Christ will come and put the final nail in the coffin of Satan, whom Christ has already conquered on Calvary.

These tell of a life beyond this one. A life where sin will no longer affect us, sorrow will cease, pain will be no more, and every tear will be wiped from the eye. Where the old will give way to the new.

To echo the hymn writer, Fanny Crosby, "Visions of rapture now burst on my sight!" The closer I get, the greater the desire grows within me for that beautiful, eternal place of rest.

It must be understood that these doctrinal truths are not all there is. God's Word is full of doctrines that the believer should hold and adhere to. It is important we read and study these so that we are fully equipped to know the difference between sound doctrine and doctrine of devils, to know the mind of God, and to apply His word to our lives. May this chapter, the ones prior, and the ones to follow stir you to allow the full Gospel light to shine brightly in you and through you.

CHAPTER

7

BEYOND APATHY

Marriam-Webster's dictionary states that apathy, impassivity, and indifference all denote a lack of responsiveness to something that might normally excite interest or emotion.

Apathy: a deadly opiate to the church, the body of Christ.

In this chapter, I will interchange "church" and "individual" or even use both at the same time. Remember, the true believer is the church. Therefore, as I often say to my own church, "If you are here, then this is for you, and, if you are reading God's word, then it is applicable to you."

Oh! How blind we get at times. How full of our self-righteousness we become. May God lay us bare to reveal to us our true spiritual state, and may we yield to His purifying power in humble repentance. Yet, so often we maintain our blinders and reject such notions of spiritual deficiency. Such is the sad state of the Laodiceans.

"And unto the angel of the church of the Laodiceans write; These things saith the Amen, the faithful and true witness, the beginning of the creation of God" (Rev 3:14).

"I know thy works, that thou art neither cold nor hot: I would thou wert cold or hot" (Rev 3:15).

"So then because thou art lukewarm, and neither cold nor hot, I will spue thee out of my mouth" (Rev 3:16).

"Because thou sayest, I am rich, and increased with goods, and have need of nothing; and knowest not that thou art wretched, and miserable, and poor, and blind, and naked" (Rev 3:17).

These are familiar to the church. We have heard sermons from this group of verses, had discussions on them, even read books (much like this one) about them. And yet, I believe it is imperative that we look into these verses once again.

The church of the Laodiceans was a church that at some point within its existence, embodied a spirit of apathy.

If you go and read before the Lord's interaction with these churches, we see the Lord described by John.

a. He is the Faithful Witness: This speaks to Jesus' utter reliability and faithfulness to His Father and to His people, even unto death. The word 'witness' could also be translated as 'martyr.'

b. He is the Firstborn of the Dead: This speaks to Jesus' standing as pre-eminent among all beings, that He is first in priority. The Body of Christ would do well to remember that He has preeminence and should be given preeminence in our lives daily.

The Firstborn among the Dead means much more than that Jesus was the first person resurrected. It also means that He is pre-eminent among all those who are or will be resurrected. As Romans 8:29 states, Jesus is the "firstborn among many brethren."

c. Prince (Ruler) over the Kings of the Earth: Before the book of Revelation is over, Jesus will take dominion over every earthly king. At present, Jesus rules a kingdom, but that is not of this world, but will be of the world to come.

Being in the Spirit, John describes what he hears and sees. He heard a voice behind him. It was a great voice. It reverberated clearly and boldly like a trumpet. This voice was clear and striking. This voice declares, "I am the Alpha and Omega." We know that this voice John hears is none other than the Lord Jesus Himself, as this is how He introduces Himself in Rev. 1:8

John gives us a glorious description of our Savior. He had heard Him and His description of Himself, now, John would turn and see His Master whom he had known during His earthly ministry.

I. He is clothed in a Garment of white: This indicates that He is a person of great dignity and authority.

II. He has a gold band around His chest: This signifies His being the High Priest, He who intercedes before the throne of God on our behalf, bearing His scars as evidence of His supreme work. While also closely inspecting the Seven Churches, for which He was responsible.

III. His head and hair were as white as wool: This signifies His unparalleled wisdom and absolute purity. Spurgeon wrote, "When we see in the picture of His head and hairs white as snow, we understand the antiquity of His reign." He is that which was, is, and will always be. He is the King of Kings and Lord of Lords.

IV. His eyes are like flames of fire: They are searching and penetrating judgment. There will be nothing which will escape His view and all will be judged according to His righteousness.

V. His feet as fine brass tried in fire: This signifies someone who has gone through the fires of judgment and come through with refined purity. Brass is strong and, therefore, speaks to stability and permanence.

VI. His voice was as the sound of many waters: His voice pierced through with power and majesty.

VII. He holds the Seven Stars in His hand: The Seven Stars as well as the Seven Candlesticks represent the Church. He holds the Church in His hands. He is holding you and me even now and keeping us!

VIII. His words are illustrated by that of a strong two-edged sword: This tells the Church that His words, all that He has spoken, are a weapon for our strength and for warring against the enemy. They are for our instruction and for our encouragement.

IX. He shines like the sun at full strength, with nothing hindering: He will never be eclipsed;

> He will never waste away. He will never be clouded. He shines bright, powerfully, and eternally. His light, which ushers from His being, will be the light of all heaven for all eternity.

Christ then, in great victory, declares…

1. Who He is: "I am He that liveth. I was dead but now I am alive forevermore!"

2. What He has conquered: "I have conquered All." He had overcome death and the grave, which once belonged to Satan, and which he used to rule with fear and torment. Now Christ has full ownership, and there will never be anyone or any way to take these away from Him.

Why is this necessary for us to fully understand? Because the Church will be judged by the risen, living, conquering, all-seeing, and authoritative Just Judge, Jesus Christ, the Risen Lord!

Now the Lord addresses the Laodiceans: His fiery eyes, from which nothing is hidden, pierce the soul of this particular church.

He views those of this church so deeply, as a sword that pierces the flesh, revealing everything that is beneath. He stares deep into the shepherd and the collective body, not measuring by their appearances, but by the spiritual vitality. The LIVING CHRIST, the Son of God, examines the life within and determines, by His own self, the vitality of this church.

After this placing them on the balances, Christ issues His judgement. LACKING! APATHETIC! INDIFFERENT!

"I know thy works, that thou art neither cold nor hot: I would thou wert cold or hot." (Revelation 3:15 KJV).

David Guzik describes this judgment this way: "In this spiritual sense, lukewarmness is a picture of indifference and compromise. It tries to play the middle, too hot to be cold and too cold to be hot. In trying to be both things, they end up being nothing — except to hear the words, 'I will vomit you out of My mouth.'"

Christ's deepest desire is to start and maintain a fervent fire inside of every believer! Yet, reality often is that we settle for an appearance, a label, and slowly we become unaware of our spiritual deficiency.

"Lukewarmness is the worst form of blasphemy" (C.H. Spurgeon).

Spurgeon preached a sermon in which he described the lukewarm church:

- They have prayer meetings, but there are few present, for they like quiet evenings at home.
- When more attend the meetings, they are still very dull, for they do their praying very deliberately and are afraid of being too excited.
- They are content to have all things done decently and in order, but vigor and zeal are considered to be vulgar.
- They may have schools, Bible-classes, preaching rooms, and all sorts of agencies; but they might as well be without them, for no energy is displayed and no good comes of them.
- They have deacons and elders who are excellent pillars of the church, if the chief quality of pillars be to stand still, and exhibit no motion or emotion.
- The pastor does not fly very far in preaching the everlasting Gospel, and he certainly has no flame of fire in his preaching.
- The pastor may be a shining light of eloquence, but he certainly is not a burning light of grace, setting men's hearts on fire.

- Everything is done in a half-hearted, listless, dead-and-alive way, as if it did not matter much whether it was done or not.
- Things are respectably done, the rich families are not offended, the skeptical party is conciliated, and the good people are not quite alienated: things are made pleasant all around.
- The right things are done, but as to doing them with all your might, and soul, and strength, a Laodicean church has no notion of what that means.
- They are not so cold as to abandon their work, or to give up their meetings for prayer, or to reject the gospel.

> They are neither hot for the truth, nor hot for conversions, nor hot for holiness, they are not fiery enough to burn the stubble of sin, nor zealous enough to make Satan angry, nor fervent enough to make a living sacrifice of themselves upon the altar of their God. They are 'neither cold nor hot' (Spurgeon).

Consider the next verse: "So then because thou art lukewarm, and neither cold nor hot, I will spue thee out of my mouth." (Revelation 3:16 KJV).

> David Guzik states, "How are churches in the mouth of Jesus?

- They are in His mouth because they spread His Word.
- They are in His mouth because He prays for them constantly.

What a terrible thing — in either of these ways — to be expelled from the mouth of Jesus!"

Whether we would like to believe it or not, Christ here shows great mercy and grace. Just as a physician shows his patient his findings, Jesus Christ begins to reveal the results of His deep examination.

"You say you are rich and increased with wealth" As I have read and re-read this section of scripture, the lesson Christ teaches in His earthly ministry makes its way to the forefront of my mind.

In looking at Luke 12, our Lord begins, "…he began to say unto his disciples first of all, Beware ye of the leaven of the Pharisees, which is hypocrisy. 2 For there is nothing covered, that shall not be revealed; neither hid, that shall not be known."

This is a fact presented throughout the Scriptures, the reality that there is nothing, nor can ever be, hidden from God. The following verses speak to this:

> "I the LORD search the heart, I try the reins, even to give every man according to his ways, and according to the fruit of his doings." (Jeremiah 17:10, KJV).

> For the word of God is quick, and powerful, and sharper than any twoedged sword, piercing even to the dividing asunder of soul and spirit, and of the joints and marrow, and is a discerner of the thoughts and intents of the heart (Hebrews 4:12 KJV).

> "The eyes of the LORD are in every place, beholding the evil and the good" (Proverbs 15:3 KJV).

> "O LORD, thou hast searched me, and known me. Thou knowest my downsitting and mine uprising, thou understandest my thought afar off. Thou compassest my path and my lying down, and art acquainted with all my ways" (Psalm 139:1-3 KJV).

Jesus goes on to give a parable:

> 15 And he said unto them, Take heed, and beware of covetousness: for a man's life consisteth not in the abundance of the things which he possesseth.

> 16 And he spake a parable unto them, saying, The ground of a certain rich man brought forth plentifully:
>
> 17 And he thought within himself, saying, What shall I do, because I have no room where to bestow my fruits?
>
> 18 And he said, This will I do: I will pull down my barns, and build greater; and there will I bestow all my fruits and my goods.
>
> 19 And I will say to my soul, Soul, thou hast much goods laid up for many years; take thine ease, eat, drink, and be merry.
>
> 20 But God said unto him, Thou fool, this night thy soul shall be required of thee: then whose shall those things be, which thou hast provided?

The rich fool's mistake was not in having wealth, but in failing to recognize that his life and soul were in God's hands. He was focused on his own comfort and security, neglecting his relationship with God and his responsibility to others.

> "The loss of a sense of need, as the drowsiness that besets a freezing man, is fatal" (Newell).

Going back to Revelation, Jesus presents to them that what they believe to be true about themselves is absolutely incorrect. They believe themselves pure, holy, righteous, and full of good works. They believe they are spiritually healthy and wealthy.

The TRUTH will reveal to them all things as He sees it and will not withhold severity in rebuke and judgement.

He tells them, "Thou art wretched, and miserable, and poor, and blind, and naked."

The Laodicean church was completely blind to this. Imagine their shock as they read this letter. Although they appeared to have it all together and had need of nothing, Jesus saw their spiritual condition. The truth behind this is that they became Apathetic. They might have had the outreaches, the preachers, the numbers, and the wealth, but they had lost the understanding of what it meant to be "poor in spirit."

Remaining poor in spirit is a call of Christ to everyone who will be in His kingdom. It is the recognition that without Him, we have nothing and are nothing. It is a recognition of our need for Him, daily.

The Laodiceans had forgotten this truth, and by forgetting this truth, they became apathetic. By becoming apathetic, they ceased being what God had ordained them to be. Inasmuch that nothing positive was said concerning them.

"Apathy is the acceptance of the unacceptable" (A.W. Tozer).

This is truly the bottom line. Apathy is the acceptance of the unacceptable, a skewed perspective of spiritual vitality, a departure from fulfilling our God ordained directives of sanctified living and global evangelization, and a blind, deceiving arrogance.

In Thom S. Rainer's book, Autopsy of a Deceased Church, He shares a story:

> I knew the patient before she died. It was ten years ago. She was very sick at the time, but she did not want to admit it. There was only a glimmer of hope at best. But that hope could become a reality only with radical change. She wasn't nearly ready for that change. Indeed, she was highly resistant to any change. Even though she was very sick. Even though she was dying. I told her the bad news bluntly: 'You are dying.' I hope I said those words with some compassion. I did feel badly sharing the news. But it was the only way I could see to get her attention. I even told her that, at best, she had five years to live. At the time I said those words, I don't really think I was that optimistic. I would not have been surprised if she died within the year. But she was not only in denial; she was in angry denial.

> 'I'll show you,' she said. 'I'll prove you are wrong. I am not dying.' Her words were fierce. Defiant. Angry. It was time for me to leave. I had done all I could. I left. I was not angry. I was sad. Very sad. Now to her credit, she was right up to a point. She did not die in five years. She proved resilient and survived another ten years. But her last decade, though she was technically alive, was filled with pain, sickness, and despair. I'm not so sure her longer-term survival was a good thing. She never got better. She slowly and painfully deteriorated. And then she died. She, of course, is a church.

An all too sad and often real. Unaware, self-absorbed, and dying. It all begins with becoming apathetic. A candle removed from its candlestick, a light vanquished by the Righteous Judge of All.

Now that I have told you what it is, I hear the words of Bro. Taylor in my Homiletics class, "Give them a way out."

The questions that we must ask ourselves are, How do we keep from becoming apathetic? Does it even matter, and, if we have become complacent, how do we get out of that dangerous pit?

If you have ever put water on the stove, the eventual and natural reaction is that the water boils; it gets hot, and it will have an effect just as it has been affected by an external force.

I preached a sermon one time entitled *Beating a Dead Horse.* The purpose was to explain the importance of reiterating what the Word of God tells the believer concerning Christian maturing, being made into the image of Christ, and spiritual maintenance.

In that message, I covered once again what I usually come around to as being necessary and important in the life of the believer. The believer should be a reader and a studier of the Word of God. The believer should frequent his personal prayer closet and join together with the body for corporate prayer. We must be faithful witnesses to the world of the power of Christ to save the broken, outcasts, and forgotten.

These are what I would consider external forces in the life of the believer that bring about and sustain a fervency that carries him from this life to the one that awaits those who endure unto the end.

Paul encouraged Christian believers in Rome along these lines.

"Not slothful in business; fervent in spirit; serving the Lord" (Rom 12:11).

This verse in Romans is in a section titled, *Marks of a True Christian.*

"Not slothful in business," "Not slothful in zeal," "Not lagging in business." In reading Romans 12:11 in various versions, this is the overwhelming call for you and me to not become complacent or to become apathetic. The Apostle Paul declares that we are to be fervent in spirit! Just like the boiling water, but constantly maintained.

This is not the only place that we have been called to be "fervent".

- FERVENT IN PRAYER: "Seeing ye have purified your souls in obeying the truth through the Spirit unto unfeigned love of the brethren, see that ye love one another with a pure heart fervently" (1Pet 1:22).
- FERVENT IN BEING PURE OF HEART: Seeing ye have purified your souls in obeying the truth through the Spirit unto unfeigned love of the brethren, see that ye love one another with a pure heart fervently" (1Pet 1:22).
- FERVENT IN CHARITY: "And above all things have fervent charity among yourselves: for charity shall cover the multitude of sins" (1Pet 4:8).

This is what it would take to keep us from becoming apathetic in our relationship with the Lord:

Maintenance. Our using the Word of God and prayer as the oxygen and fuel that brings about spiritual vitality and fervency.

Adam Clarke states, "Do nothing at any time but what is to the glory of God and do everything as unto him; and in everything let your hearts be engaged. Be always in earnest, and let your heart ever accompany your hand."

Albert Barnes gives this insight concerning being fervent, "It hence is used to denote ardor, intensity, or as we express it, a glow, meaning intense zeal, Acts 18:25." He continues, "In your mind or heart. The expression is used to denote a mind filled with intense ardor in whatever it is engaged."

This fervency in spirit is solely possible when we are transformed by the Holy Spirit. "Not by works of righteousness which we have done, but according to his mercy he saved us, by the washing of regeneration, and **renewing of the Holy Ghost."** (Tit 3:5).

The outcome of being fervent and maintaining this fervency of spirit is a desire to fulfill the command Christ gave in Matthew 28:16-20, Mark 16:15-18, Luke 24:44-49, John 20:19-23, and Acts 1:8. Not only will there be a desire to do so, but also the reciprocal effects of having fervency in spirit is an empowerment and boldness to be the witness to the world as God has ordained the church and the individual to be.

I did a study with my church on 1 Corinthians 12:1-10, 31. In this study, there was one specific point that I made often. "The evidence of the Spirit of God in the church and the life of the believer will be the miraculous." Maintaining this fervency in spirit, by the Holy Ghost, will result in miraculous things in the lives of the believers and the world.

So, what should we do if we find ourselves or our church in a state of apathy? Well, to answer this question, I will be referencing Thom Rainer's book again. On page 95 he gives four responses.

1. THE CHURCH (OR INDIVIDUAL) MUST CONFESS ITS DIRE NEED: When I consider this point, I think about Isaiah. If you have read my books or heard me preach, then you understand that Isaiah 6 is something personal and pivotal.

   We see from this text:

   - God's Holiness and Glory: The vision of the Lord on His throne, surrounded by seraphim crying, "Holy, holy, holy," emphasizes God's absolute holiness, majesty, and glory. It portrays Him as sovereign and exalted, far above human comprehension. It was in this encounter that an awful realization arose.

I have had moments for every season of my life where I am confronted with who God is and where I stand in conjunction with Him. I am reminded that outside of Him, there is nothing holy about me. I find that I am in great need. I find that it's time for me to have some spiritual growth. Often, I find myself stating the same as Isaiah did.

- Human Sinfulness and Unworthiness: Isaiah's immediate reaction—"Woe is me! for I am undone"—reveals the deep awareness of his own sinfulness in the presence of a holy God. This highlights the vast gap between divine holiness and human imperfection.

  A great disservice within the church has been portraying mankind as "not that bad." Mankind is inherently wicked. Inherently sinful. Many have been redeemed, praise the Lord for it! Yet, when we cease to remember that our old nature often desires and attempts to resurrect. When we cease to remember that we need God to not only forgive us but keep us, we begin to believe, much like the Laodiceans, "that we have need of nothing."

- Purification and Redemption: The act of the seraph touching Isaiah's lips with a live coal symbolizes cleansing and forgiveness, showing that God provides the means for purification and makes sinners fit for His service.

  I want to note at this point that, while Isaiah recognized his need and verbally acknowledged it, there was still one more step. The Seraphim came to him with a live coal to cleanse him, yet Isaiah had to submit to the cleansing, sanctifying touch.

  So often, we are confronted with our deficiency, willingly acknowledge that we are not where we need to be, but then neglect to surrender to the work that God must do to bring about this sanctification.

2. THE CHURCH (OR INDIVIDUAL) MUST PRAY FOR WISDOM AND STRENGTH TO DO WHATEVER IS NECESSARY. "If any of you lack wisdom, let him ask of God, that giveth to all men liberally, and upbraideth not; and it shall be given him" (James 1:5).

   James here is telling the Jewish believers, who had been scattered abroad (James 1:1), that the only way to gain true, spiritual wisdom was as a gift from God (vs. 5). James tells us why this is so:

WISDOM COMES FROM HEAVEN (James 3:17): Therefore it must originate from God. We must be wary of any wisdom that comes from us because it is ultimately "earthly, unspiritual," and runs the possibility of even being "of the devil" (James 3:15).

In asking for God to grant us wisdom, we are essentially asking to be able to…

- Discern God's Will: Wisdom helps individuals understand and follow God's plan for their lives (Romans 12:2). It allows them to make decisions that honor Him.

- Navigate Trials: As seen in James 1:5, wisdom is essential for enduring challenges with faith and perseverance. It provides clarity and strength during difficult times.

- Grow in Righteousness: Spiritual wisdom leads to a deeper relationship with God and a life marked by obedience, humility, and righteousness (Proverbs 9:10).

- Promote Peace and Unity: Wisdom from above is described as pure, peaceable, and full of mercy (James 3:17). It fosters harmony in relationships and communities.

- Bear Fruit for God's Kingdom: Wisdom equips believers to live in a way that glorifies God and impacts others positively, as seen in Colossians 1:9-10.

  In asking for true spiritual wisdom, we stop living for self and start living for righteousness. We start losing apathy toward the things of God and gain a fervency for that which is eternal.

  In asking God for wisdom, we literally are asking Him to show us the way back and trusting Him to do just that.

3. THE CHURCH (OR INDIVIDUAL) MUST BE WILLING TO CHANGE RADICALLY: "And be not conformed to this world: but be ye transformed by the renewing of your mind, that ye may prove what is that good, and acceptable, and perfect, will of God" (Romans 12:2).

   Radical change. This is a shift, a profound and transformative shift that fundamentally alters the way an individual or group thinks, acts, or lives. From a biblical perspective, radical change is a call to individuals who are confronted with their spiritual state. This change involves turning away from old habits, beliefs, or lifestyles to embrace God's will and purpose.

The Greek word translated as "transformed" in Romans 12:2 is μεταμορφοῦσθε (*metamorphousthe*). This word comes from the verb μεταμορφόω (*metamorphoō*), which is a compound of μετά (meta, meaning "beyond" or "after") and μορφή (morphē, meaning "form" or "shape"). It conveys the idea of a profound change, a complete reordering of one's inner character and identity, rather than merely a superficial adjustment.

Wow! The last fifteen words struck my spirit when I read them. God calls for a radical change, specifically when we are illuminated by the Spirit of Truth. He calls for us to not just "act" changed but genuinely change. "More than merely a superficial adjustment."

4. THE CHANGE MUST LEAD TO ACTION AND AN OUTWARD FOCUS: It is absolutely appropriate that this last point end the way that it does. In the last point, I told you that it is more than a superficial action. While this is true, I want to point your attention to James 2:26: "For as the body without the spirit is dead, so faith without works is dead also."

There has been much debate concerning this verse. If I may, I will take a moment to explain it in context and apply it to our current train of thought:

Many people would say that James' teaching and Paul's teaching are at odds with each other.

Paul emphasizes that our right standing with God is based solely on faith in Jesus Christ, not on obeying the law or performing human works.

"Knowing that a man is not justified by the works of the law, but by the faith of Jesus Christ, even we have believed in Jesus Christ, that we might be justified by the faith of Christ, and not by the works of the law: for by the works of the law shall no flesh be justified" (Galatians 2:16).

"Therefore we conclude that a man is justified by faith without the deeds of the law" (Romans 3:28).

Paul did not intend to downplay the importance of good works in the life of a believer. In passages like Ephesians 2:8-10 (KJV), he clarifies that while salvation is by grace through faith, believers are "created in Christ Jesus unto good works, which God hath before ordained." Here, Paul makes it clear that genuine faith will naturally produce a transformed life characterized by good works.

James emphasizes that if a person claims to have faith but does not exhibit good works, his faith is essentially ineffective and lifeless:

"What doth it profit, my brethren, though a man say he hath faith, and have not works? can faith save him?" (James 2:14).

"Even so faith, if it hath not works, is dead, being alone" (James 2:17).

"For as the body without the spirit is dead, so faith without works is dead also" (James 2:26).

True faith is one that visibly transforms a person's behavior and lifestyle.

James is not teaching that works produce salvation; rather, he's emphasizing that works are the natural fruit of a saving relationship with Christ. The transformation that occurs through genuine faith should manifest in everyday actions. The absence of such transformation raises serious questions about the authenticity of one's faith.

Quoting from Jon Courson's commentary, "James and Paul are in full agreement. It is not faith and works. It is not faith or works. It is faith that works. If your faith is real, it will show itself."

The bottom line? None of us is exempt from falling into the dangerous state of apathy. Spiritual preventative maintenance can keep us from becoming apathetic. However, if we do get into this state, there is a way out. If we have ears to hear and a willingness to open ourselves to God's Word.

Apathy doesn't have to be the finality or demise of mine or your Christian experience.

CHAPTER

8

UNAFRAID AND EMPOWERED

HOLY GHOST POWER! A phrase that is not unfamiliar to the Pentecostal church. However, along with a spirit of apathy, I believe a spirit of fear and forgetting has permeated the church.

There is a statement that I heard growing up: "What one generation does in moderation, the next will do in excess." I have seen a downward progression. Ignorance from not being taught. This younger generation is in many ways unaware of the potential that can happen with a life that is completely consecrated and empowered.

Henry Varley, a British evangelist, stated this phrase to D.L. Moody who then not only lived to become this but also preached it: "The world has yet to see what God can do with a man fully consecrated to him." It is becoming harder to find men and women who will do this and live this.

A powerful verse, spoken by our Savior, speaks to us plainly:

"But ye shall receive power, after that the Holy Ghost is come upon you: and ye shall be witnesses unto me both in Jerusalem, and in all Judaea, and in Samaria, and unto the uttermost part of the earth" (Acts 1:8).

I want us to understand that we are not a powerless people. I want us to understand that we are not weak, as the world would portray us. We may experience intense pressures from the enemy and from our flesh, but we are not without resources.

I want us to understand that we are not simple-minded, backwoods, or ignorant. I want us to understand that, because our identity is found in Christ and through His promise, by the infilling of the Holy Ghost we are endued with Power! Power in the Greek is "dunamis," from which we get our word dynamite.

When Christ says we are going to receive power, He means explosive, powerful in effect, and great potential. If you looked up dynamite in the dictionary, it is primarily attributed to destruction and conflict;

however, when the Holy Ghost gets involved, the only thing destroyed is the powers of darkness!

Dr. E.V. Hill's 1992 conference sermon stated:

> 10 to 15 years ago, when J. Edgar Hoover was head of the FBI, he invited a number of leaders, some 200 or more, to New York to discuss the plight of our country as it related to subversive activities. He invited us to hear about the left-wing and the right-wing movements in the United States. And, so all of a sudden with these 200 people on the 40th floor at the Hilton Hotel, they began to discuss the Black Panther party and its impact upon New York City. That the Panthers have New York, the Panthers were roaming the streets of New York. The Panthers had shut up all stores after 5:00 o'clock in Harlem, New York and upper New York. The Panthers had closed down the Central Park for the most part, the Panthers made millions of people cross the bridges hurrying out of New York. The Panthers had fear-gripped New York City, millions of people, nearly four million people fled because the Panthers were on the march. So, I asked Mr. Sullivan a question. I knew the answer, but I wanted everybody else to know it. I said, Mr. Sullivan, how many Panthers are active in New York? How many

> of them are causing stores to be locked up? How many of them are causing churches not to have worship at night? How many of them are closing down Central Park at night? How many of them have gripped the town with fear? What is the active membership of the Black Panther party of New York? Mr. Sullivan said, "81." 81 running four million people across the bridges. 81 closing down churches and businesses. 81 causing fear to grip and shutting down the places of social activity. Just 81.

You want to know the difference between them and us? E.V. Hill brings this out: They so believed in their ideology that they were willing to die for it. You want to know why the early church thrived and had the testimony that they turned the world upside down? They loved not their lives unto death.

My desire, throughout this whole book, has been to convince and encourage the believer that we have power by the Holy Ghost! We don't have to live a spiritual life that is superficial, weak, and quickly demising.

I would like you to keep in mind two things:

- The Holy Ghost is promised: "But ye shall receive power, after that the Holy Ghost is come upon you: and ye shall be witnesses unto me both in

Jerusalem, and in all Judaea, and in Samaria, and unto the uttermost part of the earth" (Acts 1:8).

I had a kid in our Christian school one time make this statement: "I believe that if God has been consistent in keeping His promises to His people throughout history, He will do the same concerning the promise of the infilling of the Spirit."

I can confidently declare, as did Joel the Prophet and Peter the Apostle, that God is a keeper of His promises and that the promise of the Holy Ghost is for you and me.

- Receiving hinges upon our obedience: "And we are his witnesses of these things; and so is also the Holy Ghost, whom God hath given to them that obey him" (Acts 5:32).

Those who obey God are not just passive believers but active participants in His work, receiving His Spirit as confirmation and empowerment.

Throughout Acts, obedience is often tied to the spread of the Gospel and the work of the early church. The apostles, despite opposition and persecution, remained steadfast in their mission, and their obedience allowed them to experience God's power firsthand. This verse suggests that obedience is not merely following rules but aligning one's life with

God's will, which opens the door to a deeper connection with Him.

I want to look at four reasons why the power of the Holy Ghost is given:

I. For the preaching of the Gospel:

> And said unto them, Thus it is written, and thus it behooved Christ to suffer, and to rise from the dead the third day: And that repentance and remission of sins should be preached in his name among all nations, beginning at Jerusalem. And ye are witnesses of these things. And, behold, I send the promise of my Father upon you: but tarry ye in the city of Jerusalem, until ye be endued with power from on high (Luke 24:46-49).

These, of whom Christ had invested in for three and a half years, would become empowered by the infilling of the Holy Ghost on the day of Pentecost. He told them the purpose of this empowerment would be for the primary reason of spreading the gospel. Even under the extreme pressure of persecution, it was the power of the Holy Ghost that enabled them to stand fast in the faith and continue in spreading the good news of Jesus to the world.

II. For the warring of spiritual battles: We know the scripture, "we wrestle not against flesh and blood." However, if I may present this to you, we don't recognize the spiritual from the physical because we have not been recently endued with Power, or it has been some season since we've tapped into that power.

I was a freshman at Ozark Bible Institute and was traveling with the Choir then. I remember a conversation I had with the bus driver. We were discussing spiritual things, and he made this statement, "Demonic activity has not changed. The problem is, the church does not have enough of the power of the Holy Ghost to discern when there is demonic activity. The church does not have enough power of the Holy Ghost to make war against them."

The Holy Ghost reveals what and who we fight. We are told that in Ephesians 6:11:

Put on the whole armour of God that ye may be able to stand against the wiles of the devil. (Ephesians 6:12) For we wrestle not against flesh and blood, but against principalities, against powers, against the rulers of the darkness of this world, against spiritual wickedness in high places.

We are even told that we have been given the "equipment" required to make war:

> Wherefore take unto you the whole armour of God, that ye may be able to withstand in the evil day, and having done all, to stand.
>
> Stand therefore, having your loins girt about with truth, and having on the breastplate of righteousness;
>
> And your feet shod with the preparation of the gospel of peace;
>
> Above all, taking the shield of faith, wherewith ye shall be able to quench all the fiery darts of the wicked.
>
> And take the helmet of salvation, and the sword of the Spirit, which is the word of God:
>
> Praying always with all prayer and supplication in the Spirit, and watching thereunto with all perseverance and supplication for all saints (Eph. 6:13-18).

Christ, the Baptizer of the Spirit, tells us in Luke ?:19: "Behold, I give unto you power to tread on serpents and scorpions, and over all the power of the enemy: and nothing shall by any means hurt you."

David Guzik states, "Because Satan was fallen and the disciples were messengers of Jesus and His kingdom, they enjoyed the superior power of God over Satan."

As His followers, we have been given the same power and authority over the enemy. As Christ has overcome, so can we.

III. For the working of signs and wonders:

> "And now, Lord, behold their threatenings: and grant unto thy servants, that with all boldness they may speak thy word" (Acts 4:29).
>
> "By stretching forth thine hand to heal; and that signs and wonders may be done by the name of thy holy child Jesus" (Acts 4:29).
>
> "And when they had prayed, the place was shaken where they were assembled together; and they were all filled with the Holy Ghost, and they spake the word of God with boldness" (Acts 4:31).

They prayed for power to be used by God in miracles! Adam Clark states:

> This power they received from the Holy Spirit, who enabled them, μεγαλῃ δυναμει, (great power), with striking miracles, to give proof of the resurrection of the Lord Jesus; for this is the point that was particularly to be proved: that he was slain and buried, all knew; that he rose again from the dead, many knew; but it was necessary to give such proofs as should convince and confound all.

I preached a series on the gifts of the **Spirit**, from 1 Corinthians 12, at my church. In that series, I made this statement. "The proof of the Spirit of God in the church is evidenced by the miraculous." I want to add to this statement I made by stating, this includes the proclamation of the Gospel with an anointing, from the throne of God, that causes the hardened heart to become softened unto repentance and the saint rejoice at hearing it.

IV. IT IS FOR ALL THAT BELIEVE: "For the promise is unto you, and to your children, and to all that are afar off, even as many as the Lord our God shall call!" (Acts 2:39).

David Guzik in his commentary stated concerning this verse,

> "As they repented and demonstrated faith and obedience by baptism, the gift of the Holy Spirit would be given to them as it was given to the original group of disciples. Peter also specifically promised that the promise of the Holy Spirit would be given to those who believe in all succeeding generations (all who are afar off)."

All believers are entitled to, should ardently expect, and earnestly seek the promise of the Father, the baptism in the Holy Spirit and fire, according to the command of our Lord Jesus Christ.

This was the normal experience of all in the early Christian Church. With it comes the enduement of power for life and service, the bestowment of the gifts and their uses in the work of the ministry.

Three evident things concerning the Holy Ghost

1. It is for you! The Holy Ghost was given to individuals. Individuals of different backgrounds and professions. God is no respecter of persons.

2. It is for your children! There is no age limit to being filled with the Holy Ghost. I remember being in Corpus Christi at a youth camp. I remember being in the services where little children ages four and up being filled with God's Spirit!

3. It is for all, no matter your race, creed, nation, or dialect. The baptism of the Holy Ghost is for all born-again believers! I have been in foreign countries and seen the very same Spirit of God that filled me, reside and work in believers there!

With the baptism in the Holy Spirit come such experiences as…

1. an overflowing fullness of the Spirit:

   "In the last day, that great day of the feast, Jesus stood and cried, saying, If any man thirst, let him come unto me, and drink.

   He that believeth on me, as the scripture hath said, out of his belly shall flow rivers of living water.

   (But this spake he of the Spirit, which they that believe on him should receive: for the Holy Ghost was not yet given; because that Jesus was not yet glorified)" (John 7:37-39).

2. a deepened reverence for God:

   "And fear came upon every soul: and many wonders and signs were done by the apostles" (Act 2:43).

3. an intensified consecration to God and dedication to His work,: "And they continued stedfastly in the apostles' doctrine and fellowship, and in breaking of bread, and in prayers." (Act 2:42).

4. a more active love for Christ, for His Word and for the lost: "And they went forth, and preached every where, the Lord working with them, and

confirming the word with signs following. Amen." (Mar 16:20) .

Why is it important to "Be filled with the Holy Ghost?"

1. He enables us to live as righteous and faithful life to God.

2. He comforts us and intercedes for us in trying and spiritually hard times.

3. Our children need examples of what it means to be Holy Ghost filled and Fire Baptized! My son knows more about paw patrol than he does the Holy Ghost. Young people today know more about famous TikTok celebrities, sports stars, and movie references than they do about the Holy Ghost.

4. He enables us to witness and share the Gospel with the lost.

5. He empowers us to withstand, resist, and overcome the enemy when He tries to attack us, our homes, or our churches. Sadly, we can barely discern when the Spirit speaks to us, much less when devils are in our presence.

I have often told my church people, "Even more than you desire to be filled and empowered, God desires to give that to you!" I say the same to you,

Dear Reader. The Lord, who is faithful in all of His promises, is calling for you and me to be His people, to have Him fully possess our lives. Empowering us for greater.

"For I know the thoughts that I think toward you, saith the LORD, thoughts of peace, and not of evil, to give you an expected end" (**Jeremiah 29:11**).

"Cast not away therefore your confidence, which hath great recompence of reward. For ye have need of patience, that, after ye have done the will of God, ye might receive the promise" (**Hebrews 10:35-36**).

The hope that awaits those who are surrendered and endure to the end is a lively one. So, don't lose heart, Saint of God. Stay the course.

The purpose of this entire book has been to remind, convict, and encourage the believer, the church, and even myself to arise to what God has ordained us to be and to be faithful in it until the end.

He has plainly given us a design that we should follow. It requires sanctified living, obedience to His Word, and being empowered for service.

May we do this:

Heavenly Father,

We come before You with hearts full of gratitude and reverence. We thank You for the gift of the Holy Ghost, which empowers us to live righteous lives and be witnesses for Christ. Lord, we acknowledge that You have ordained the church to be a beacon of light, hope, and truth in this world.

We pray for a fresh outpouring of Your Spirit upon us. Fill us with Your power, wisdom, and boldness. Help us to rise up and embrace the calling You have placed on our lives. May we be unafraid and empowered to preach the Gospel, wage spiritual battles, and work signs and wonders in Your name.

Lord, we ask that You remove any fear, doubt, or complacency from our hearts. Strengthen us to stand firm in our faith and to be courageous in the face of challenges. Let us be biblical, let us be sanctified, let us be your church. Let us be witnesses for Christ, shining brightly in a world that desperately needs Your love and truth.

Father, we commit ourselves to you.

In Jesus' name, we pray. Amen.

In a world where the light of faith often flickers, this book was written as a call. A calling upon all believers to reignite their spiritual fervor. This compelling book delves into the essence of true Christianity, urging readers to embrace the fullness of God's Word and live out their faith with unwavering commitment.

Through insightful teachings on church leadership, discipline, and doctrine, To the Children of Light, challenges the modern church to return to biblical principles and become the vibrant, empowered body of Christ it was meant to be. Whether you're a seasoned believer or new to the faith, this book offers a transformative journey towards spiritual maturity and a deeper understanding of God's purpose for His church.

Thomas R Hammond Jr, a fourth-generation minister and author of *Confidence In The Call and Character of Kingdom Citizens*, has been involved in ministry all of his life. His fervent passion is to re-establish biblical truth in an unbiblical world, to reach the lost, and with a great desire to mentor the next generation of the church and its ministers.

To be spent for Christ:

He and his family live and serve as Pastors at Faith Heritage Tabernacle in Southeast, Texas.

About Kharis Publishing:

Kharis Publishing, an imprint of Kharis Media LLC, is a leading Christian and inspirational book publisher based in Aurora, Chicago metropolitan area, Illinois. Kharis' dual mission is to give voice to under-represented writers (including women and first-time authors) and equip orphans in developing countries with literacy tools. That is why, for each book sold, the publisher channels some of the proceeds into providing books and computers for orphanages in developing countries so that these kids may learn to read, dream, and grow. For a limited time, Kharis Publishing is accepting unsolicited queries for nonfiction (Christian, self-help, memoirs, business, health and wellness) from qualified leaders, professionals, pastors, and ministers. Learn more at: https://kharispublishing.com/

www.ingramcontent.com/pod-product-compliance
Lightning Source LLC
La Vergne TN
LVHW010614100826
845148LV00014B/2962

* 9 7 8 1 6 3 7 4 6 6 7 2 8 *